Lida B Miller, A. R White

Delightful Bible Stories for our Young Christian Endeavorers

Lida B Miller, A. R White

Delightful Bible Stories for our Young Christian Endeavorers

ISBN/EAN: 9783337172831

Printed in Europe, USA, Canada, Australia, Japan

Cover: Foto ©Lupo / pixelio.de

More available books at **www.hansebooks.com**

CHRIST BLESSING LITTLE CHILDREN.

Delightful Bible Stories

FOR OUR

Young Christian Endeavorers,

And All Who Believe in the Blessed Truths Set Forth in Holy Writ, and who Delight in the Marvelous Stories of the Book of Books. Especially adapted to the use of Homes, Sunday Schools and Epworth Leagues.

Embellished with a Wealth of Illustrations in Wood Engraving, Depicting Bible Scenes, with Eight Specially Designed Lithographs in Ten Colors.

EDITED BY

LIDA BROOKS MILLER and ANNIE R. WHITE,
Assisted by REV. HOYT BAILEY.

PUBLISHED ONLY BY

MONARCH BOOK COMPANY,
Formerly L. P. MILLER & CO.,

OLD TESTAMENT STORIES.

TABLE OF CONTENTS.

1. The Creation	9	
2. The Fall of Man	13	
3. Cain and Abel	17	
4. The Flood	22	
5. Abraham, or the Promised Land	31	
6. Abraham	35	
7. Abraham, or the Trial of Love	38	
8. Jacob or the Heavenly Dream	42	
9. Jacob, or the Long Journey	51	
10. Jacob, or the Meeting	55	
11. Joseph, or the Pit	60	
12. Joseph, or the Slave	66	
13. Joseph, or the Prisoners	70	
14. Joseph, or the Butler and Baker	72	
15. Joseph, or the Release	76	
16. Joseph, or the Ruler of Egypt	81	
17. Joseph, or the Feast	86	
18. Joseph, or the Forgiving Brother	91	
19. Joseph, or the Long-lost Son	96	
20. Moses or the Basket of Bulrushes	100	
21. Moses, or the Pious Choice	107	
22. Moses, or the Burning Bush	111	
23. Moses, or the First Plagues of Egypt	117	
24. Moses, or the Last Plagues	121	
25. Moses, or the Red Sea	127	
26. Moses, or the Manna and the Rock	133	
27. Moses, or Mt. Sinai	137	
28. Moses, or the Golden Calf	142	
29. Moses, or the Tabernacle	148	
30. Moses, or the Priests	152	
31. Moses, or the Journeys of the Israelites	156	
32. Moses, or the Twelve Spies	158	
33. Moses, or the Sin of Moses and Aaron	162	
34. Moses, or the Serpent of Brass	165	
35. Moses, or the Death of Moses	168	
36. Joshua or Rahab	173	
37. Joshua, or the River Jordan	177	
38. Joshua, or the Walls of Jericho	182	
39. Joshua—His Death	187	
40. Samuel, or the Pious Mother	190	
41. Samuel, or the Little Prophet	195	
42. Samuel, or the Ark in Battle	198	
43. Samuel, or the God Dagon	201	
44. Saul, or the King	205	
45. Saul, or the Disobedient Deed	208	
46. David, or the Young Shepherd	211	
47. David or the Harp	213	
48. David, or the Giant Goliath	215	
49. David, or the Javelin	227	
50. David, or the Cave	226	
51. David, or the Spear	230	
52. David, or the Promise Fulfilled	233	
53. David, or the Ark on Zion	237	
54. David, or Uriah's Wife	241	
55. David, or the Punishment	246	
56. David or the Oak-tree	250	
57. David, or the Farewell	254	
58. Solomon, or the Wise Choice	256	
59. Solomon, or the Temple	259	
60. Solomon, or the Queen's Visit	263	
61. Solomon or the Idols	267	
62. Jeroboam or the Dried up Hand	269	
63. Elijah, or the Ravens	271	
64. Elijah, or the Widow	274	
65. Elijah, or the Two Altars	278	
66. Elijah, or the Rain	284	
67. Elijah, or the Call of Elisha	288	
68. Elijah, or the Vineyard of Naboth	291	
69. Elijah or the Three Captains	295	
70. Elijah, or the Chariot of Fire	298	
71. Elisha, or the Bears	301	
72. Elisha, or the Little Room	303	
73. Elisha, or the Little Maid	309	
74. Hezekiah, or the King who Trusted in God	314	
75. Nebuchadnezzar, or the Golden Image	316	
76. Belshazzar, or the Writing on the Wall	320	

I will instruct thee and teach thee in the way which thou shalt go: I will guide thee with mine eye.

OLD TESTAMENT STORIES.

CHAPTER I.

THE CREATION.

My Dear Children: I know that you have heard that God made the world. A man could not make such a world as this.

Men can make many things, such as boxes and baskets. Suppose you were to shut a man up in a room which was empty and say, "You shall not come out till you have made a box." Would the man ever come out? No, never. A man could not make a box, unless he had something to make it of. He must have some wood, tin, pasteboard, or something. But God had nothing to make the world of. He only spoke, and it was made.

Making things of nothing is called "creating." No one can create anything but God.

God is called the Creator because He created all things. There is only one Creator. Angels even cannot create things. They could not create one drop of water, or one little fly.

God was six days in creating the world.

On the first day, God said: "Let there be light;" and there was light. And God called the light Day, and the darkness Night.

On the second day, God spoke again, and there was water very high; that water is called the clouds. There was also water very low. There was nothing but water to be seen. God filled every place with air; but you know the air cannot be seen.

THE CREATION.

On the third day, God spoke, and the dry land appeared from under the water; and the water ran down into one deep place. God called the dry land Earth, and the waters Seas. We walk upon the dry land. We cannot walk upon the sea. God spoke, and things grew out of the earth. Grass and corn, and trees and flowers.

On the fourth day, God spoke, and the sun and moon and stars were made. God ordered the sun to come every

No. 5. Fifth Day of Creation.

morning, and to go away in the evening. It is best that it should be dark at night, when we sleep. But God lets the

THE CREATION.

No. 6. Sixth Day of Creation.

moon shine, and the stars also; so that if we go out in the night, we often have a little light. There are more stars than we can count.

On the fifth day, God began to make things that are alive. He spoke and the water was filled with fishes, and birds flew out of the water, and perched upon the trees.

On the sixth day, God spoke, and the beasts came out of the earth; lions, sheep, cows, horses, as well as all kinds of creeping things, such as bees, ants, and worms.

At last God made a man. God made man's body of the dust, and then breathed into him. The man had a soul as well as a body. So the man could think of God. And afterward God made the woman from a piece of the flesh and bone from the man's side.

God gave all the other creatures to Adam and Eve; He blessed them, and put them into the garden of Eden, and told Adam to take care of the garden.

When God had finished all His works, He saw that they were good. He was pleased with the things He had made. They were all beautiful. The light was glorious; the air was sweet; the earth was lovely, clothed in green; the sun and moon shone brightly in the heavens; the birds and beasts and all the living creatures were good and happy; and Adam and Eve were the best of all, for they could think of God and praise Him.

You know there are seven days in the week. Now, on the seventh day God did not make anything; He rested from all His works. He called the seventh day His own day, because He rested on it. This is the reason people rest on the seventh day, and call it God's day. It is the Sabbath-day.

CHAPTER II.

THE SIN OF ADAM.

You remember that God put Adam and Eve in a pretty garden. There they lived very happily. They were kind to each other; were never sick nor in pain. Adam worked in the garden, but not so hard as to tire himself. His work was pleasant, for it was never too hot nor too cold, and there were no weeds nor thistles growing.

There was one tree of which Adam might not eat. The name of the tree was: The tree of the knowledge of good and evil.

God said, that if Adam ate of it, he should die. Adam and Eve might eat of all the other trees in the garden.

They loved God. He was their friend, and used to walk and talk with them.

You know there are a great many wicked angels; one of them is called Satan. This wicked angel wished to make them unhappy, so he thought: I will try and persuade them to eat that fruit which God has told them not to eat. So Satan put on the body of a serpent, and came into the garden.

He saw Eve, and pretended to be kind, and said: Why do you not eat of the fruit?

But she said: God has told us not to eat of that fruit; if we do, we shall die.

But the serpent said: No, you shall not die, but this fruit will make you wise like God.

THE SIN OF ADAM.

The woman was afraid to eat; but she looked, and thought the fruit nice; she looked again, and thought it pretty. So she took the fruit and ate it, and gave some to Adam.

By eating they became sinful; they knew they had done

No. 7. The Temptation.

wrong; they were afraid of seeing God. Soon they heard His voice in the garden, and they went and hid themselves among the thick trees, that grew all over the garden. But they did not hide them from God.

God called Adam, and said: Adam, where art thou?

Adam and Eve.

Then Adam said: I was afraid, and hid myself.

Then God said: Have you eaten of that tree?

Then Adam said: The woman gave me of the tree, and I did eat.

God said to the woman: What is this that thou hast done?

And she said: The serpent deceived me, and I did eat.

God was angry with them all, but most of all with the serpent. God said to him: You shall always crawl on the ground, and eat dust.

Then God said to the woman: You shall often be sick, and Adam shall be your master, and you must obey him.

And God said to Adam: You shall work hard, and dig the ground; thorns and thistles shall grow; you shall have bread to eat, but you shall be obliged to work so hard that drops of sweat shall stand upon your forehead; you shall be sad while you live, and at last you shall die; your body was made of dust, and it shall turn into dust again.

How sad Adam and Eve must have felt when they heard this. But this was not all; they were not allowed to stay in the pretty garden. God drove them out, and would not let them come into the garden again; so He sent an angel with a fiery sword to stand near it.

CHAPTER III.

CAIN AND ABEL.

After Adam and Eve were turned out of the garden, they had two little children—Cain and Abel.

Cain was wicked like Satan, but Abel was good. Abel was always sorry for his sins, and asked God to forgive him.

Cain and Abel had to work hard like Adam their father. Cain dug the ground and planted trees. Abel took care of sheep; he was a shepherd.

ADAM AND EVE AFTER THE EXPULSION.

God did not walk and talk with people then, as He had done in the garden; but He spoke sometimes, and allowed people to pray to Him.

God wished them always to remember Him, so He taught them a way of keeping it in their minds.

SACRIFICES OF CAIN AND ABEL.

He told them to pile up large stones—this heap was called an altar—then to put some wood upon the altar, and take a lamb, or a kid, and bind it with a rope to the altar; then to take a knife and to kill the lamb; and then to burn it. Doing this was called "offering a sacrifice."

CAIN.

When people did this, God wished them to think how He would one day let His Son die for their sins.

Abel brought lambs, and offered them up to God; and Abel thought of God's promise; so God was pleased with him. But Cain did not obey God, but brought fruit instead of a lamb; so God was displeased with Cain, and did not like his sacrifice.

Then Cain was very angry, and hated Abel, because he was good, and because God loved him best.

Then God said: Why are you angry? If you will love and serve me, I shall be pleased, but if not, you shall be punished.

Still Cain went on in wickedness. Now hear what he did at last. One day he was talking with Abel in a field, when he rose up and killed him.

Abel was the first man that ever died. You see Cain began by hating Abel, and ended by killing him, though he was his brother.

Soon Cain heard the voice of God calling. God said: Where is your brother Abel?

I know not, answered wicked Cain; am I my brother's keeper?

But God said: I have seen your brother's blood upon the ground; and you must be punished. You shall leave your father and mother, and wander about on the earth.

Cain said: My punishment is greater than I can bear.

But he went and lived a great way off, and built houses for himself and his children.

So Adam and Eve lost both their sons in one day; Cain

went a great way off, and Abel died. How they must have wept as they put dear Abel in the ground. But they must have wept still more to think that Cain was so wicked.

But God had pity on Adam and Eve, and gave them another son, who was good; he was called Seth.

The children of Seth feared God; and God loved them, and called them His children.

CHAPTER IV.

THE FLOOD.

Cain had a great many children; Seth had a great many children.

At last Adam and Eve died, and Cain died, and Seth died; but still there were a great many people in the world.

NOAH BUILDING THE ARK.

At first some were good, but at last they all were wicked, except one man: his name was Noah.

THE ARK.

THE FLOOD.

God was very angry with the wicked people, and determined to punish them.

God said to Noah, I will make it rain so much that all people shall be drowned, except you, and your wife, and your children.

Then God told Noah to make a great ark.

An ark is like a covered boat or ship. Noah made a very great ark, which would swim upon the top of the water, when God should drown the wicked people.

Noah made the ark of wood, cut down trees, and cut boards, and then fastened them together. He made one door in the ark, and one little window at the top.

Then he told the people that God was going to drown the world, and advised them to leave off their wickedness.

But they would not mind. They went on eating and drinking, not thinking of God, or trying to please Him.

God did not choose that all the beasts, birds and insects should be drowned; so he told Noah to get some birds, some beasts, and some insects of every sort, and to bring them all into the ark. God could make all these animals go quietly in. Noah put corn, fruit and grass into the ark, for them to eat.

So Noah got some birds of every sort; doves, ravens, eagles, sparrows, larks, robins, and many others, and they flew in at the window. He also got some beasts of every kind, sheep, horses and dogs; and he got insects of every kind, butterflies, ants and bees.

All these went into the ark; for God made them gentle and obedient. Then Noah himself went in, with his wife, his three sons, and their wives. Eight people in all were in

RETURN OF THE DOVE.

the ark. But Noah did not shut the door: God shut the door, and Noah knew that he must not open it till God bade him.

Then it began to rain. It rained day and night. How the wicked people must have wished that they had minded Noah! If they climbed trees, the water soon reached to the tops; if they went up high mountains, the water rose as high as they; for it rained forty days and forty nights. All beasts and birds and men and children died, except those that were in the ark.

At last nothing was to be seen but water, and the ark floating upon the top of the water. Noah lived in the ark almost a whole year.

A long while after it had left off raining, Noah wished to know whether the waters were dried up. He went among his birds and choosing a raven, let it out of the window. A raven is a fierce bird. It did not like the ark; though there were no trees to be seen, nothing but water, yet the raven would not go back to Noah, but went on flying night and day over the water.

When Noah saw that the raven did not come back, he went among his birds, and chose a dove. A dove is a gentle bird. Noah put it out at the window; and when it saw nothing but water, the dove came back. Noah knew when his bird came back—it pecked at the window—and he put out his hand and pulled it in.

Noah waited seven days, and then he sent the dove out again; and this time the dove saw some trees. Yet the dove did not stay, but plucked off a leaf with its beak, and came back. Noah must have loved his good little dove for coming back to him again.

Noah waited seven days more, and then he sent out the

COMING OUT OF THE ARK.

dove again, and this time it did not come back. Now Noah knew that the earth was dry, but he waited in the ark till God told him to go out.

THE FLOOD.

At last God said: Go out of the ark, you and your wife, your three sons and their wives, and the birds, the beasts, the insects, and all the creeping things.

When the door was open, the beasts came out. How glad the sheep must have been to lie down again upon the soft grass, and the goats to climb the high hills.

When the window was open, the birds flew out. How glad they must have been to perch again among the trees.

MT. ARARAT.

Noah saw all the green hills and fields again; but where were all the wicked people? He would never see their faces again.

Noah remembered God's goodness in saving him from being drowned. He made a heap of stones for an altar; he took some beasts and birds, and offered a sacrifice to God.

Then God made a kind promise to Noah. He said: I will

NOAH'S SACRIFICE.

never drown the world again. When it rains, do not think there will be a flood. Look up in the sky after the rain, and you will see a bow. That shall be the sign that I remember my promise.

What beautiful colors a rainbow has. It puts us in mind of God's kind promise not to drown the world any more.

TRAINED DOVE.

CHAPTER V.

ABRAHAM, OR THE PROMISED LAND.

Noah's sons had many children, and they had many children, until at last there were a great many people in the world. These people were bad. They did one very wicked thing. They cut down trees, and made the wood into little

images like dolls, and kneeled down and prayed to the images, and said: These images are our gods.

All of them spoke one language. But they grew to think less and less about God, and finally resolved to build a great tower, and in this way make themselves a great name.

So they laid the foundation of an enormous tower, and built upon it until it was very high. But it was never finished, for God was not pleased, and he confused their language so they could not understand each other.

ABRAHAM, OR THE PROMISED LAND.

The name of the tower was Babel, which means confusion. There are ruins to this day near the river Euphrates, which are thought to be those of the Tower of Babel.

Most of the people in the world worshiped idols, instead of the true God. Sometimes these idols were made of wood and sometimes of stone, or silver, or gold.

God looked down from heaven, and saw the people worshiping idols, and He was very angry.

Then God said: I will choose one man, and teach him to love and be my servant. Now there was a man called Abraham. His father and his friends worshiped idols. God said to Abraham: Leave your own home and friends, and go to a country which I will show you; and I will bless and take care of you.

Abraham did not know where God would tell him to go; yet he went because he was obedient.

Abraham had a wife called Sarah, whom he loved very much. Sarah went with him. He took some sheep, cows and servants.

There were very few houses to be seen; only fields and trees. Abraham slept in a tent. He made the tent with long sticks, covering it with skins of beasts.

He could move his tent from place to place; over high hills

BUILDING BABEL. (AFTER NOAH.)

and wide rivers. At last he came to a beautiful country called Canaan, full of trees, flowers, grass and corn. This was the place that God chose for him to live in.

Sometimes he made a heap of stones, called an altar, and offered sacrifices to God. Abraham never worshiped idols; but all the people in Canaan did.

God often spoke to Abraham, and said: I will bless you and take care of you. God was pleased that Abraham had left his own home when He told him to, without asking a question.

ANIMALS USED FOR SACRIFICE.

CHAPTER VI.

ABRAHAM, OR THE PROMISED CHILD.

Abraham and Sarah lived in a tent in the land of Canaan. They had no little child. Abraham was very old, and Sarah was very old too. They were both much older than your grandfather and grandmother. Abraham was almost one hundred, and Sarah was almost ninety.

One night God said to Abraham: Come out and look up to the sky. The sky was full of stars, more than could be

THE PROMISE TO ABRAHAM.

counted. God said: You shall have a great many grandchildren and great-grandchildren, and they shall have more children, and they too, shall have more children, till there are as many people as there are stars in the sky; and they shall live in the land of Canaan, and the wicked people shall be turned out.

Now Abraham had not even one little child; yet he believed that God would do as He had promised.

One day Abraham was sitting in his tent. It was about twelve o'clock, and very hot. He looked up, and saw three men. He ran to meet them, and said: Pray come and rest yourselves, and let me bring a little water to wash your feet, and a little bread for you to eat.

These men were angels, though they looked like men. They had come from heaven with a message. Angels are often near us, though we cannot see them.

The angels sat outside under the tree. Sarah was in the tent. Abraham said to Sarah: Take some flour, make some cakes, and bake them quickly. Then Abraham took a fat calf, and said to a servant: Kill it, and roast it quickly.

When it was ready the three men began to eat.

While they were eating, they said to Abraham: Where is Sarah? Abraham said: She is in the tent. Then one of the men said: Sarah shall have a son.

Sarah heard what the angel said, and she could not believe that she would *really* have a child given to her, now she was so very old; so she laughed to herself.

The next year Sarah's little son was born. His name was Isaac. He was a good child, and God loved him. Abraham and Sarah were much pleased with their little son.

THE ANGEL APPEARING TO ABRAHAM.

CHILDREN OF BETHEL.

CHAPTER VII.

ABRAHAM, OR THE TRIAL OF LOVE.

At last, Isaac grew up to be a man. He also lived in a tent. They all three loved God, and loved each other very much. It was a happy little family.

Abraham was a very rich man. He had cows, horses, sheep and goats, tents and servants, silver and gold. But he had one thing that he loved more than these. That was his son, his dear son Isaac.

Yet there was one Being whom Abraham loved even better still. That was God.

At last, God said He would try Abraham, to see whether he loved Him more than *any thing* in the world—more even than he loved his son Isaac.

You have heard how Abraham used to burn lambs upon altars. Now God said to Abraham: Take your dear son Isaac, and offer him up on an altar in a place that I will show you.

This was a very hard thing for Abraham to do. But Abraham wished to do all God told him, because he loved God so much. So Abraham cut down some wood to burn; he told two of his servants and Isaac to come with him. He left Sarah in the tent at home. They all four walked on for three days; at last they saw a high hill a great way off.

Abraham knew that was the place where he was to build the altar; so he said to his servants, Stay here while Isaac and I go and worship God. He took the wood and bound it round

ABRAHAM AND ISAAC.

Isaac with a rope. Then he took some fire and a knife, and Abraham and Isaac walked up the hill together.

Isaac did not know that his father was going to offer him as

THE SACRIFICE OF ISAAC

a sacrifice; he thought that his father would offer a lamb. So he said, Father. Abraham answered, Here am I, my son. And Isaac said, Here is fire and wood; but where is the lamb? My son, said Abraham, God will find a lamb. But Abraham did not tell Isaac that he was to be the lamb, and the boy expected to find one.

At last they came to the top of the hill. Then Abraham took stones, and built an altar; and he took the wood off Isaac's back, and laid it on the altar. Now the time was come when Isaac must know who was to be the lamb. The rope that had bound the wood was fastened round the hands and feet of Isaac, and he was laid upon the wood like a lamb.

Then Abraham took the knife, and lifted up his hand to kill Isaac, when he heard a voice calling, Abraham, Abraham! It was an angel speaking from heaven. The angel said: Do not kill your son, or hurt him at all; for now God knows that you love him, because you have given Him your only son.

How glad was Abraham to untie the rope that bound Isaac, and to find that he need not kill him.

Abraham saw a lamb caught in the bushes; and he took it, and offered it up as a sacrifice instead of Isaac. Abraham thanked God very much for having given him back his son, and the angel called to him out of heaven again, and said: God is much pleased with you for having given up your son; and God will bless you and all your children and grandchildren, and their children, and one of your children's children shall make all people happy.

When the angel had done speaking, Abraham and Isaac went down the hill together—there was no wood now on Isaac's back.

They found the servants where they had left them, and they all went back together to Sarah.

CHAPTER VIII.

JACOB, OR THE HEAVENLY DREAM.

In time Abraham and Sarah became very old. At last Sarah died, and Abraham wished to bury her, but he had not a piece of ground in Canaan to bury her in; so he gave some of his silver to the people in Canaan, and bought a field.

The field was full of trees, and there was a cave in it. Abraham took the dead body of Sarah, and put it in the cave.

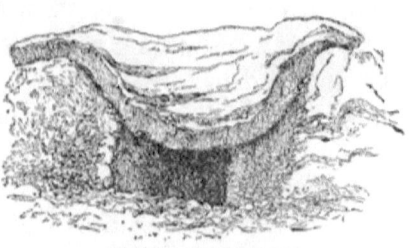

ANCIENT JEWISH TOMB.

Abraham now knew that God would soon take him away from this world, so he wished to see his son happily married, but was very much puzzled to know where to find him a wife, for Isaac was forty years old, and had never asked any woman to marry him. In those days fathers could force their sons to do whatever they ordered, and if a man became a grandfather, he was almost a king in his family. Abraham didn't like the young women of the country in which he lived, so he determined to find a wife for his son in another country in which most of his earlier life had been spent. The old man was too feeble to go there himself, and he was afraid his son might make a mistake if he went, so his head servant agreed to go, and he was sent to this distant country with camels and rich presents of gold and silver. This was a very odd errand, to

REBEKAH AT THE WELL.

go and hunt a wife for another man, for most men like to look around for themselves, if they intend to marry.

ANCIENT WELL.

Well, this old servant at last reached the edge of a city in the land he was sent to, and he saw a large well there with cold, delicious water in it, and a number of young women filling their leather bottles, and carrying them into the city to their homes. His master had told him that God had sent His angel on before him to help him to select the proper woman; and this was true, for in a few minutes after the servant's arrival at the well, a beautiful young woman came up to draw water, and she allowed the servant to drink out of her bottle, and then she filled the trough with water, that all of his camels might drink also.

After the camels had taken a good long drink of water, the old servant asked this kind young girl where she lived in the city, and whether her father would let him sleep in his house, and let his camels be fed in his barn. He gave her gifts of gold, and found that she was one of his master's distant relations. She invited him to the house, and treated him very kindly. When they reached the

EASTERN PITCHERS.

ISAAC GOING OUT TO MEET REBEKAH.

house, the old servant told her mother and brother that he wished her to go to the country he had come from, and marry his young master.

CARRYING WATER.

I once knew a young lady who went all the way to England, from this country, to marry the gentleman to whom she was engaged; but, of course, she had known him very well before and loved him deeply; but just think of it, this beautiful maiden, about whom I am writing, said that she was willing to leave her mother and her home, and travel right off, without delay, to another land to marry a man she had never seen, nor had she even heard of him until that day. God's angel must have whispered something to her to induce her to make such a journey. All this time the young master was wondering what sort of wife was to be brought to him; and late one afternoon, as he was taking a walk, he saw the camels returning home, and one of them had a young woman sitting on its back, but she had veiled herself, and he could not tell what she looked like. Then he took her into the tent in which his dear mother had died some years before, and she removed her veil from her face, and he made her his wife, and they were a very happy couple, I assure you.

EASTERN WOMEN VEILED

At last Abraham died, and Isaac his son buried him in the same cave where Sarah lay.

Isaac and Rebekah had two little sons. They were called Esau and Jacob. They were twins; that is they were of the same age. Their faces were unlike, and their hearts were unlike. Esau was wicked; but Jacob was good, and loved God. When Esau was a man, he became a hunter. He had a bow and arrows; he used to go into the woods and hunt game, and bring it home, and dress it for dinner; and he gave some of the meat to his father Isaac.

Jacob was a shepherd: he staid at home near his tent with his father and mother, and his sheep and goats. He loved God, and prayed to God very often.

I am sorry to tell you that Isaac loved wicked Esau better than he loved good Jacob.

But Rebekah loved her son Jacob, and God loved Jacob, and God was not pleased with Esau. Do you think that Esau and Jacob loved one another?

They did not. Jacob sometimes behaved unkindly to Esau. One day Esau said: My father will soon die, and then I will kill my brother Jacob.

Rebekah heard that Esau meant to kill Jacob some day; so she was frightened, and called Jacob, and said to him: Your brother Esau means to kill you. Go to your uncle, who lives a great way off, and stay with him. Soon Esau will leave off being angry; then I will send for you.

Jacob did as his mother advised. He took leave of his father. Jacob did not ask his father to give him anything. He took no servant with him, no sheep, not even a horse to ride upon. He only took a stick in his hand, and set out on his journey. Jacob felt very sad. He was a poor stranger, and was going to a far country which he had never seen.

He had no tent, nor house to sleep in by the way; so when night came, he took some stones for a pillow, and lay down to sleep on the ground. There were bears and wolves, but God took care of him. God knew how sad he was, and made him dream the sweetest dream that you ever heard.

JACOB'S DREAM.

In his sleep Jacob saw a great many steps reaching up to the sky, and on the steps beautiful angels; some going up, and some coming down: and at the top he saw God Himself. Then Jacob heard a voice, and God spoke to him, and said: I am the God of Abraham, and of Isaac, and I will take care of you wherever you go; and I will bring you home again, and your children shall live in this land of Canaan, where you are sleeping.

Then Jacob awoke out of his sleep, and knew that God and His angels were watching over him. He wished never to forget the place where he had this sweet dream; so he took the stones which had been his pillow, and made them into a heap. Now, he thought, I shall be able to find the place when God lets me come back to Canaan.

TOMB OF RACHEL.

CHAPTER IX.

JACOB, OR THE LONG JOURNEY.

Then Jacob went on his journey. He traveled many days. At last he came to a place where there was a great deal of grass. In that place there was a well, with a great stone upon the top of the well. Many sheep were round the well; and men were with the sheep. These men were shepherds. There was very little water in that country where Jacob was.

Jacob said to the shepherds: Do you know a man called Laban?—that was the name of his uncle.

Yes, said they, we do.

Then Jacob said: Is he well?

The shepherds answered: He is well; and here is his daughter Rachel coming with the sheep.

Jacob was very glad to hear this, for Rachel was Jacob's cousin. He ran to her and kissed her, and wept.

Jacob had not seen a friend for a long while, and he was glad to see his cousin.

Rachel did not know who Jacob was, till he said: I am your cousin, and am come from a great way off.

Then Rachel said to her father: My cousin Jacob I found sitting by the well.

Then Laban was glad, and ran out to meet him; he kissed him, and said: You must come to my house: I am your uncle.

Jacob's Uncle Laban had two daughters, one of whom was very pretty, while the elder one was plain. Jacob wanted to marry his pretty cousin, and his uncle agreed to the marriage.

JACOB'S WELL.

if he would work seven years for him. So Jacob took charge of his uncle's sheep and goats, and at the end of the seven years he asked for his cousin to be given him in marriage. But the uncle told him he must first marry the elder daughter, and at the end of seven years more he would give him the younger daughter also, for in those days a man could have a number of wives. So Jacob labored for seven years more,

RACHEL AND JACOB AT THE WELL.

and then married his younger cousin also. So Jacob had two wives. People must not have two wives now; but then they might have two wives, and even more than two.

God gave Jacob a great many little children. I will not tell you their names, because there were so many. Jacob lived a long while in tents with his wives and his little children. He took care of Laban's sheep; but Laban gave him sheep and goats for his own. Jacob had plenty of bread to eat and raiment to wear, as God had promised; for God *always* keeps his promises.

But Jacob could not forget his father and mother, and Canaan. Here he had lived when he was a little boy.

EASTERN SHEEPFOLD.

CHAPTER X.

JACOB, OR THE MEETING.

At last Jacob said to Laban his uncle: I have been your servant a long while, and now I want to go home.

FLIGHT OF JACOB.

Once, while Jacob was taking care of the sheep in the field, he fell asleep, and had a dream, and in his dream he heard God say to him: Go home to your father, and I will be with you.

When Jacob awoke, he sent a servant to call Rachel and Leah, for he wanted to speak to them; and he said: God has spoken to me in a dream, and told me to return to my father.

Then Rachel and Leah said: We will go with you.

Then Jacob packed up all his things—his tents, clothes and furniture. He put his things on the backs of his camels, placed his wives and children on camels too. He told his servants to drive all his sheep, cows, goats and camels. So they all set out.

Jacob was pleased to go back to Canaan; but there was one thing that frightened him. He remembered that Esau had once said that he would kill him; and he was afraid lest he should now come and kill him and his children.

Soon Jacob heard that Esau was coming with four hundred men. Jacob thought Esau was coming to kill him: so he began to pray to God, and said: O God, Thou hast been very kind to me, and given me a great many things; do not let Esau come and hurt me, and kill my wives and my little children. Thou didst promise to take care of me. God heard Jacob's prayer.

Jacob thought to himself, I will send a present to show Esau that I wish to behave kindly to him. So he took a great many goats, sheep and cows, and told his servants to tell Esau that he had sent them as a present.

In the morning Jacob looked up and saw Esau coming, and four hundred men with him. Jacob did not run away; but went up to Esau.

Esau put his arms around Jacob's neck and kissed him, and they both wept. God had made Esau's heart more kind.

How glad Jacob was to find his brother so kind. Jacob prayed to God to make him kind, and God had heard his prayer.

Esau looked up, and saw Rachel and Leah and the little children; and Esau said: Who are these?

And Jacob said: These are my children.

MEETING OF JACOB AND ESAU.

Then Esau said to Jacob: I met a great many sheep, and cows, and goats; why did you send them on before you?

Jacob said: They were a present for you.

Esau answered: I have enough, my brother; keep what you have for yourself.

Pray take my present, said Jacob, for God has given me a great deal. And Jacob begged Esau so much to take it, that at last he did.

Esau said to Jacob: Let us take our journey together; and I will go on first.

ESAU DEPARTING.

But Jacob said: I cannot go as fast as you, for I have many little children, young lambs and goats; and if one day we were to drive them too fast, they would die.

Then Esau went home to his own house, which was a great

way off; for Esau did not live in Canaan. But Jacob staid in the land of Canaan, for he wished to live there.

You see that God let Jacob come back to Canaan, as He had promised. Jacob did not forget the sweet dream I told you of. He went to that very place once more: he had made a heap of stones to mark the place, so that he could find it again. There he built an altar, and offered sacrifices to God, who had been so very kind to him. God had given him food and clothes, as He had promised, and He had given him many more things besides; He had given him wives and children, and servants, and cattle; and God had made his brother kind to him.

ANCIENT ALTAR.

CHAPTER XI.

JOSEPH, OR THE PIT.

Jacob saw his old father, Isaac, again; and then Isaac died, and Jacob and Esau buried him.

Jacob chose to live in Canaan, with his children and his cattle.

All the sons were grown up to be men except Benjamin, who was still a little babe. Joseph was older than Benjamin. He was a big boy, and the best of all the children. The ten

JACOB'S ARRIVAL IN EGYPT.

JOSEPH'S DREAM.

eldest were wicked. They used to take care of sheep and goats; and when Joseph was with them, they grieved him by their wicked behavior; they were unkind to him, and spoke roughly. Jacob loved Joseph the best, and this made the others envious. They hated him because he was the pet and the darling.

Jacob loved Joseph too much. He gave him a pretty coat made of many colors, yellow, blue, green, pink, red, purple; and Joseph used to wear it.

One night Joseph had a very strange dream. He thought he was in a field of corn with all his brothers, and were making up large bundles called sheaves. He thought each of his brothers made a sheaf, and that all his brothers' sheaves bowed down to his sheaf. Joseph thought this a very strange dream, and he told it to his brothers.

But when they heard it they were angry, and said: We suppose you mean that we shall bow down to you. And so they hated him still more.

Soon after Joseph had another strange dream. He thought he saw the sun, moon, and eleven stars in the sky, and that they bowed down to him. This dream was more strange than the other, and he told it to his father as well as to his brothers.

His father was surprised, and said: Does the sun mean me, and the moon your mother, and the stars your brothers; and shall we bow down to you?

Yet Jacob thought that God had sent the dream to Joseph, and would make it come true; but the brothers were more and more angry.

JOSEPH, OR THE PIT.

Now Joseph's brethren had a great many sheep and goats to take care of, and there was not enough grass for them all round the tents; so they took their flocks a great way off, that they might eat fresh grass. Joseph staid at home with his

SUN, MOON AND STARS.

father; and Benjamin staid at home, because he was such a little child.

At last Jacob wished to know how his sons were; so he said to Joseph, Go and see your brothers, and come and tell me how they and the flocks are.

Joseph was always ready to do what his father wished; so he set out on his way. He took no servant, but putting on

JOSEPH APPROACHING HIS BROTHERS.

his pretty coat, he wished his dear father good-bye. He little thought how long it would be before he should see him again.

Joseph went a great way, but could not find his brothers. At last a man saw him, and said: For whom are you looking?

And Joseph answered: I am looking for my brothers; can you tell me where they are?

Now the brothers saw Joseph coming, and they said to each other, Here this dreamer comes; let us kill him, and throw him into a deep pit, and tell our father that a lion or a bear has eaten him up.

When Joseph came up they seized hold of him.

The brothers were going to kill him, when one of them named Reuben said: Do not kill him, but only throw him into a pit. This brother was a little kinder than the rest, and meant to take him out and bring him back to Jacob. But they first took off his pretty coat.

Oh! how bitterly he cried when he saw what they were going to do to him; how he begged them to spare him, and to let him return to his father! But they would not hear, for their hearts were harder than stone.

They threw him into the deep, dark pit; there he lay. hungry and thirsty and weary, without one drop of water to quench his thirst. How it must have grieved Joseph to think that he should not return to his dear father; and his father perhaps would think that he was dead.

The wicked brothers cared not for his groans, but they sat down and began to eat their dinner.

CHAPTER XII.

JOSEPH, OR THE SLAVE.

While the brothers were eating their dinner, they looked up and saw some people coming. As they came nearer, they saw camels, and men riding them.

These men lived in the country a great way off, and had been to some hills where some very costly things grew, called spice and balm. They had plucked these things, and had put them in large bundles on the backs of their camels. They were going to carry them to a country a great way off, and sell them for money.

This was their way of getting their living, and it was a good way; yet they were wicked men, as you will see.

One of the brothers named Judah, said: Let us sell Joseph; for it would be better to sell than to kill him: we shall get some money if we sell him; and it would be cruel to kill him.

The other brothers said that they thought it was a good plan. So they called to the men, and asked if they would buy a young boy.

And the men said: Yes. We will give you twenty pieces of silver for him.

The brothers pulled Joseph out of the pit. Perhaps he thought they were going to let him return to his father.

Poor Joseph! He soon found that his brothers were not going to be kind. The men paid the money, and took Joseph and carried him away.

When Joseph was gone, the brothers said: What shall we

JOSEPH'S COAT DIPPED IN BLOOD.

tell our father? We will not say we have seen Joseph, but will say we have found his coat on the ground.

Then the brothers killed one of their goats, and dipped the pretty coat in the blood. We will show our father this coat, said they. So they carried the coat home, all covered with blood.

Jacob had been thinking of his sons while they were gone. How glad he must have been when he heard the bleating of their sheep, and knew they had come. He looked to see whether Joseph was with them. But no. His sons came up to him. In their hands they held a bloody coat. They showed it to Jacob, and said: We have found this. Do you think it is your son's coat?

Jacob knew that coat, and said: A lion or bear has eaten him up, and has torn Joseph to pieces.

How Jacob wept for his darling child! How sorry he was that he had sent him alone to seek his brothers! The wicked brothers tried to comfort Jacob, and said: Do not weep so much. But Jacob would not hear.

No, I shall die, and then I shall be with Joseph; for I shall never be happy any more.

How sad it was for this old man, leaning on his staff, his hair gray, and his face full of sadness, while he thought that his dear boy had been eaten up. His little Benjamin was a comfort to him; Jacob would never let him go away, nor would he trust him with his brothers, though he did not know how wicked they had been.

JOSEPH'S COAT.

CHAPTER XIII.

JOSEPH, OR THE PRISONER

The men who had bought Joseph, took him to Egypt.

When they got there they sold him as if he had been a horse or a cow. In some countries men are sold, and are called slaves. Poor Joseph was sold as a slave. There was a very rich man, and he bought Joseph for a slave. His name was Potiphar. He took Joseph home with him. He did not send him to work in the field, but made him a servant in the house. So Joseph had no very hard work to do.

Joseph tried to be a good servant. Though he wished to be with his father, he did not waste his time fretting, but took great pains to please his master. When his master told him to do anything, he did it so well that his master was pleased with him. It was God who made Joseph able to do his work well; and Joseph's master knew that it was God that helped him to do things well. I suppose Joseph had told him; for his master did not know the true God, but worshiped idols.

His master liked him better every day. At last, he said to Joseph, I can trust you so well that I will give you the charge of the other servants when I am out. Take care of the house, and all the things in it, of the garden and of the fields; for I can trust you.

So Joseph had the care of everything. He behaved the same as if his master were watching him; for he knew the eye of God was always upon him. There are many children who behave ill as soon as their parents go out of the room: such children do not fear God.

Though Joseph had the care of nice things to eat, and beautiful things to wear, he only took what his master allowed him to take. God made the things grow well in the field, and the work to go on right in the house, so that Potiphar had no trouble himself, but found that Joseph would manage all for him.

Joseph had now all he could wish for; but he could not forget his father, and his little brother Benjamin.

Now Potiphar had a very wicked wife. She wished poor Joseph turned out of the house; for he had found out how bad she was, and so she did not like to see Joseph.

This wicked woman said to Potiphar: Your slave, that you think so good, is wicked, and when you are out he behaves very ill.

Potiphar was so foolish as to believe her, and he said: Joseph shall be put in prison.

There were a great many men in the prison, and most of them had done very bad things, but Joseph had done nothing wrong. God still loved Joseph, and he could make him happy, even in a prison.

At last the keeper took the chains off Joseph's feet, and allowed him to walk about the prison, and take care of the prisoners. The keeper found that he could trust him, and that Joseph managed things well.

CHAPTER XIV.

JOSEPH, OR THE BUTLER AND BAKER.

The prison was in the house of Potiphar. One day, Potiphar brought two men to Joseph, and said to him: Take great care that these men do not get out of prison. I give them under your charge. You see Potiphar thought Joseph could be trusted; perhaps he had found out that Joseph was not so bad as he had once thought.

JOSEPH INTERPRETING THE DREAMS

These men were the servants of the king of Egypt. The king of Egypt had a great many servants to wait on him. One of his servants used to bring him wine in a cup to drink. This servant was called his butler. Another used to bake things for his dinner. He was called the baker.

The butler and the baker had both offended the king: I do not know what they had done, but they were shut up in prison.

Then Potiphar brought them to Joseph, and told him to

keep them safe. Joseph shut them up in a room together, and gave them bread and water every day, and took care of them.

One morning when Joseph came to see them, he observed that they looked very sad. He said to them: Why do you look sad?

They answered: We have each had a strange dream to-night, and we think our dreams have some meaning, but we cannot find it out; and there is nobody in the prison who can tell us.

Then Joseph said: But my God knows all things; he could tell me the meaning. Only tell me your dreams.

The butler told his dream the first. He said: I thought I saw a tree such as grapes grow upon —*a vine*. It had three branches, but no grapes. While I was looking, I saw little buds, and they turned into grapes, and they grew ripe. I picked the grapes, and squeezed them into a cup, and made wine, and then brought the cup to the king for him to drink.

THE BUTLER'S DREAM.

This was the butler's dream, and God told Joseph the meaning of it.

You saw three branches, said Joseph; something will happen you in three days. The king will send for you to be his butler again.

When the baker heard this pleasant meaning, he thought that his dream would be pleasant too; so he began to tell it. The baker said: I dreamed that I was carrying three white baskets on my head, the one on the top of the other. In the baskets there were baked meats and birds came and picked the meat out of the top basket.

Something will happen to you in three days, said Joseph. The king will send for you, and will hang you upon a tree, and the birds will pick your flesh off your bones.

THE BAKER'S DREAM.

So while the butler was pleased with what Joseph had told him, the poor baker was sorry, because he knew that he must die.

Joseph had one little favor to ask of the butler. Tell the king I am shut up in prison, and cannot get out. I once lived in a land a great way off, and was stolen, and now I am shut up in this prison, though I have done nothing wicked. Beg the king to let me out.

You see Joseph did not tell of his brothers' wickedness in having sold him.

In three days the king sent men to the prison for the butler and the baker. It was the king's birthday, and he had made a feast for his servants, and he had thought of the butler and baker, and had said: Let the butler come back to me; and let the baker be hanged; I will not forgive him. So now both the butler and the baker knew that Joseph had told them the truth.

The butler forgot to tell the king about Joseph. I suppose he was thinking of the fine things he saw, of eating and drinking, of money and clothes. The butler was unkind, and worse than unkind; he was ungrateful.

Poor Joseph waited in vain. No one came to let him out of prison. One day passed, and then another — summer came, and then winter, but Joseph was still shut up. Yet God had not forgotten him.

SACRED OX.

CHAPTER XV.

JOSEPH, OR THE RELEASE.

I have told you of the great king of Egypt. His name was Pharaoh. He had a great many servants. He sat upon a throne, wore beautiful clothes, a chain of gold around his neck, a ring upon his hand, and a crown upon his head. He lived in a fine house, and rode out in a fine chariot drawn by many horses; and as he passed by, people bowed down to the ground. One night, this great king had two very strange dreams.

He thought he was standing by a river, and seven fat cows came out of the river, and began to eat the grass. This was a pleasant sight; but, soon after, he saw seven very thin cows come out of the river, and they ate up the seven fat cows; and yet, after they had eaten them, they looked as thin as they did before. Then the king awoke.

But soon he fell asleep, and dreamed that he saw a stalk of corn with seven fine ears growing on it. While he was looking he saw another stalk with seven very bad ears of corn on it; and these bad ears ate up the seven good ears.

These were Pharaoh's two dreams. He thought them strange, and longed to know their meaning. In the morning he told his servants to find some one who could tell the meaning of dreams. A great many men came who pretended to be wise; but they could not tell the king the meaning of his dreams.

At last the butler thought of Joseph, and said: You know,

O king, that you were once angry with me and with your baker, and you shut us up in prison. While we were in prison, the baker and I each had a dream, and a young man told us the meaning of our dreams, and said that the baker would be hanged, and that I should be let out of prison; and so it was,

PHARAOH HONORS JOSEPH.

just as the young man had said. Then Pharaoh told his servants to bring this young man out of prison.

So the servants came to the prison for Joseph. Joseph must have been glad to hear this, but he was dressed in very poor clothes, not fit for a king to see. So the servants gave him neat clothes.

It was a long, long while since Joseph had felt the sweet air blow upon his face, and had seen the green fields. He looked pale and sick.

He came into the king's fine house, and stood before him. The king said, I hear that you can tell the meaning of dreams.

It is not myself, said Joseph, that can tell the meaning, but my God can. Then Pharaoh told Joseph his two dreams.

When he had done speaking, Joseph answered: Both your dreams have the same meaning. This is what is going to happen. The next seven years a great deal of corn will grow in the fields; but afterward hardly any corn will grow for seven years. The seven fat cows mean the seven years when much corn will grow; and the seven thin cows mean the seven years when very little corn will grow. God sent you these dreams, that you might know what is going to happen.

Now what could the king do? First there would be a great deal of corn, then scarcely any. Joseph gave the king some advice. He said: Save up some of the corn when there is so much, that you may have some when there is none growing. You should look for a very wise man, who will save up the corn, and put it in large barns; or the people will die when no corn grows in the fields.

Pharaoh was much pleased with Joseph for telling him the meaning of his dreams; he believed what Joseph said. And the king said: Joseph shall save up the corn.

Then Pharaoh said to Joseph: You are so very wise that you shall help me to manage all the people in the land. Every one shall mind you as they do me, and you shall be the greatest person next to me.

CONCERT IN EGYPT.

Then Pharaoh took the ring off his hand, and put it on Joseph's hand; and he gave him beautiful clothes, and a gold chain to wear round his neck. He gave him a fine chariot to ride in, and told the people to obey him.

So Joseph was made a great ruler; but he would not be idle. He went about all the country in his chariot to get corn, and built large barns, and filled them with corn, and so he did for seven years.

He was glad he was out of prison, and thanked God very much. He was not happy because he wore fine clothes; but he was glad to be able to do good to people, by saving up corn. He married a wife, and had two little boys; yet still he thought of his dear old father, and hoped that he should one day see him again; and he thought of little Benjamin, and he hoped that his brothers were sorry for their wickedness. He did not feel angry with them for the great wrong they had done him.

CHAPTER XVI.

JOSEPH, OR THE RULER OF EGYPT.

A great deal of corn grew in the fields next year and the year after, and for seven years then scarcely any corn grew. The poor people came to the king and said: We have nothing to eat, and Pharaoh said: Go to Joseph; he can help you. So the people went to Joseph, and he opened his large barns full of corn, and sold the corn to the people. They brought money, and large bags or sacks. Joseph took the money, and filled the sacks with corn. A great many people came to buy corn: some from a long way off; but Joseph had enough corn for all.

Among the people who came, there were ten men who had come from a far country. Who do you think these were? They were Joseph's brothers. When Joseph saw them he remembered them, though he had not seen them for twenty years. He knew those cruel brothers who had sold him for twenty pieces of silver. If he pleased, he might have punished them.

The brothers thought Joseph was a great ruler, and they did not know that they had seen him before; for he wore fine clothes, and he was grown to be a man, and he had another name, which the king had given him.

So, when the ten brothers saw him, they bowed upon the ground. Then Joseph remembered his dream about the sheaves bowing down to his sheaf, and he saw that God had made it come true.

JOSEPH, OR THE RULER OF EGYPT.

Joseph felt ready to forgive his brothers; but he wished first to see whether they were sorry for their wickedness, and whether they loved their father and little Benjamin. Joseph did not tell them who he was. He even pretended to be

AND JOSEPH KNEW HIS BRETHREN.

unkind. He spoke to them in a rough voice, and said: Where do you come from?

From the land of Canaan, they said; to buy food.

But Joseph said he did not believe they spoke truth. You come, he said, to see what a bad land this is, with no corn growing, and you mean to bring some king with soldiers to fight us.

No, indeed, said Joseph's brothers, we do not. We are ten poor brothers, and we have come to buy food.

But Joseph pretended he would not believe what they said.

Joseph's brothers answered: We are all brothers, and once there were twelve of us, but one is dead, and the youngest is with our father, who is an old man. They tried to make Joseph believe what they said, but he would not; that is, he pretended not to believe them.

At last Joseph said: I must see your youngest brother. I shall send one of you to bring him, and I shall keep the rest in prison till he comes back with the youngest brother.

The brothers knew their father would not part with Benjamin. So not one of the brothers said he would go and bring Benjamin.

Joseph put them all in prison, and kept them shut up together for three days. While they were shut up, they had time to think.

At last Joseph came to them and said: This is what you must do, and then you shall live; for I fear God.

How glad and surprised the brothers must have been when they heard him say he feared God; for the other people in Egypt worshiped idols.

Joseph said: I will keep only one of you shut up in the prison; all the rest of you may go back, and take corn home with you; but when you come again, you must bring your youngest brother with you, or I shall think you have not spoken truth; but if you do bring him, I will believe you.

The brothers were glad to think they might go back, yet it

made them sad to hear that one of them would be kept in prison.

Joseph heard what they said, and it made the tears run down his cheeks; so that he was obliged to go out of the room to weep. He did not like to see them unhappy; but you know he wanted to find out whether they were kind to Benjamin, and if they loved their aged father, and were sorry for all they had done.

When Joseph came back, he took one of the brothers, called Simeon, and said that he would keep him in prison till the others brought their youngest brother with them. So Joseph had Simeon bound with ropes, or chains, while the other brothers stood round.

Then they must have remembered how once poor Joseph had been bound, and sold for a slave.

Simeon was left alone in the prison, and he did not know whether his brothers would ever come back, or whether he would ever be let out.

Before the brothers set off to go home, Joseph said to his servants: When you fill those men's sacks with corn, put back into their sacks the money that they paid me for it, and give them also some food by the way.

When they were come home, they told their father all that had happened. There was a great ruler they said, who sold corn to the people; and he spoke very roughly to us, and said that we were not come to buy corn, but that we only wanted to see the land, that we might bring men to fight the poor hungry people that lived there. He called us spies. We told him that we were not spies, but were twelve brothers; that one was dead, and that one was with our father in the land of Canaan. But he would not believe us, and told us we must bring our youngest brother with us; and he took Simeon, and shut him up in prison, and said that he would not let him out till we came back with Benjamin.

Poor old Jacob was very sorry when he heard this. Then the brothers began to open their sacks of corn, and were surprised to find their money at the top of their sacks; but they were not pleased; they thought that some one had put the money there to get them in disgrace, and that when they went back to Egypt, they should be punished for stealing.

They were more afraid than ever of going back to Egypt, and seeing the great ruler; yet they wished very much to go, for they had only bought a little corn, and they wanted more; and they knew that poor Simeon would remain in prison till they went back.

Jacob said: No, I cannot trust Benjamin with you, lest some harm should happen to him. You have taken away two of my children, Joseph and Simeon. If any evil were to happen to Benjamin, you would bring down my gray hairs with sorrow to the grave. Jacob felt that it would break his heart to lose Benjamin, he loved him so very much.

So the brothers were obliged to stay in Canaan; for they knew it would be of no use to go to Egypt, unless Benjamin went with them.

CHAPTER XVII.

JOSEPH, OR THE FEAST.

But soon they had eaten up all their corn, and none grew in their fields.

Jacob saw how hungry they were, and at last he said: Go again, buy us a little food.

Then they said: We cannot go without Benjamin; for the man who sold corn said we should not see him, unless we brought our youngest brother. If you let Benjamin come with us, then we will go.

Jacob said: Why did you tell the man you had a brother?

Then the brothers answered: The man asked us so many questions. He said to us: Is your father alive? Have you another brother?

Still, Jacob did not like to let Benjamin go.

One of the brothers called Judah, said, I will take care of Benjamin, if you will let him go. I promise to bring him back to you.

Jacob saw it was of no use to refuse any more. So he gave Benjamin into the care of Judah.

But Jacob was afraid of the man being unkind to them, and of his saying they had stolen the money. So he said to them, Carry the man a present.

Pick some nuts and almonds off your trees, said Jacob; and take a little balm and myrrh, and some spices, and a little honey with you as a present.

The man was very rich, and did not want anything, but

the present would show him that they wished to please him, and do right.

Besides, said Jacob, take the money back that you found in your sacks; take more money in your hands to buy more corn, and take Benjamin, and go to the man.

Jacob's heart was full of pain when he said this. Then he began to pray to God.

When Jacob wished his dear Benjamin good-bye, he thought of how he once had parted with his Joseph, the day he sent him to look for his brothers, when he put on his pretty coat.

The brothers took the present, and they each took some money in their hands, and they took their asses, and their empty sacks; and Judah took care of Benjamin.

So they parted from their old father, and their wives, and their little children, and they set out on their journey.

They all felt very sad that day. They were afraid they should be taken up as thieves when they got to Egypt.

At last they came to Egypt. They went to the place where Joseph was selling the corn. He looked to see whether Benjamin was with them. How pleased he was.

Benjamin was very young when Joseph had seen him last, yet Joseph knew him.

As soon as he saw his brothers, he called his servant, who managed his house, and said: Take those ten men to my house, and get a great dinner ready; for they must dine with me to-day.

The brothers did not understand what Joseph said to the servant, for he spoke in another language. The servant came and told them to come with him. So he brought them to Joseph's own house, a fine large house. Yet the brothers were not pleased, but very frightened.

Ah! said they, we are going to be put in prison; and we shall be kept in Egypt, to work hard.

They thought of their poor father, and of what he would do.

When they got to the door of the house, they came up to the servant, and said: O sir! we came here once before to buy a little food, and we paid money for it; but when we got home we opened our sacks, and found the money in them, and here we have brought it back; and we have brought more money to buy more corn. We cannot tell who put the money in our sacks.

The servant answered them very kindly, and said: Fear not.

How happy the brothers were now! They soon found that they were not going to be put into a prison, but that they were to dine in a fine house. What could make the man so kind?

While they were waiting, the servant went and brought poor Simeon out of prison. He had been shut up a long while.

The servant told them that dinner would not be ready till noon; and while they were waiting, he brought them water to wash their feet, and gave some food to their poor tired and hungry beasts.

The brothers said: Let us get our present ready, while we are waiting for the master to come.

So they went out, and got ready the balm and spices, the honey, and nuts, and almonds.

At last Joseph came, and the brothers came into the house,

OFFERING JOSEPH THE PRESENT.

and brought the present, and they bowed down upon the ground.

This time Joseph spoke very kindly to them. He asked how they were; but most of all he wanted to know how his dear father was.

Is your father well? he asked; the old man of whom you spoke? Is he yet alive?

They said: Yes, our father is well, and he is alive.

Then Joseph looked for Benjamin, and when he saw him, he longed to throw his arms round his neck, and kiss him, but he would not do it yet. He only said: Is this your younger brother that you told me of?

And then he made this little prayer: God be gracious to thee, my son.

When Joseph had said this, he felt the tears coming into his eyes, and he could not help crying; so he went into his own room, and there he cried. He was a very tender-hearted man, and he loved this young brother very much.

Now the dinner was ready; so Joseph would not stay in his room; but washed his face, that no one might see that he had been crying; and tried to look cheerful.

In the room where they were to dine, there were three tables. One was for Joseph's servants, another was for Joseph himself—for he always dined at a table by himself—and the other table was for the eleven brothers.

Joseph told them where to sit; he made the eldest sit first, and then the second, just according to their age, and he made Benjamin sit last. The brothers were surprised at Joseph's knowing which was eldest and which was second, for it is hard to tell how old a grown-up man is; but Joseph knew them better than they thought he did.

Now they all sat down to dinner. It was long since they had such a dinner, and they had made a great journey, and were tired and hungry and thirsty.

Joseph could see them all, and it was a pleasant sight. Once they had eaten their dinner while he lay in the pit, and they had given him none. Yet he would not treat them so, but would return good for evil.

CHAPTER XVIII.

JOSEPH, OR THE FORGIVING BROTHER.

The brothers spent a happy day with Joseph. They did not go home that day, but waited to set out on the morrow.

You know that they had come to buy corn, and they had brought empty sacks with them. Joseph called his servant, and said to him secretly: Fill the sacks of those eleven men with corn, and put their money that they have given me for the corn back into their sacks. And put my silver cup into the sack of the youngest.

The servant filled the sacks with corn, and put the money nto them. And he put the silver cup into Benjamin's sack. They did not know that the servant had put money and a cup into them.

The next morning, as soon as it was light, the brothers rose up, took their beasts and their sacks, and set off to return home to their father. How glad they were to get away safely, not one left behind!

What a pleasant history they should have to tell their father! How much surprised he would be to hear of the great man's kindness, and how glad he would be to see Benjamin again!

But soon was all their joy turned into grief.

They had gone but a little way, when some one called them. It was Joseph's servant; he came running after them.

What made you, said he, behave so ill to my master, after all his kindness to you? Why have you stolen his silver cup?

The brothers were much surprised to hear that the cup was stolen. We would not do such a thing, they said. Did we not bring back the money, when we thought it had been put in our sacks by mistake? And now would we steal a silver cup? None of us have taken it.

Then the servant told them to open their sacks: so the eldest brother took down his sack; the servant looked in among the corn, but could find no cup. Then the second opened his sack, but there was no cup hid in it. The third showed his, and each brother showed his in his turn. At last Benjamin showed his. How much were they all surprised when they found the silver cup in it.

You know that Benjamin had not stolen it. You know that the servant had put it in the sack when he filled it with corn.

The servant said to Benjamin: You must come back with me to my master. He was going to take him for a slave, and never let him return home; but he said that his brothers might go home.

And would they go and leave Benjamin behind?

No, said they, we will go back with Benjamin.

You see that they loved Benjamin, and they would not leave him alone in his distress.

They put their sacks again on their beasts, and followed the servant to Joseph's house. Their hearts were bursting with grief, and they cried as they went.

Joseph was in his house waiting for them.

Joseph was glad to see them all come back with Benjamin. Now Joseph saw that they loved Benjamin.

Joseph spoke to them as if he was angry, and said: What is this wicked thing that you have done?

You remember that Judah had promised to take care of Benjamin. So Judah began to beg Joseph to forgive Benjamin.

Judah knew that it would be of no use to say that Benjamin had not taken the cup, so he only begged Joseph to take pity on them.

God is punishing us for our sins, said Judah, and we can say nothing; we must all be your slaves.

No, said Joseph, not all, only he who stole the cup; he shall be my slave; let the others go back to their father.

Joseph wanted to see whether the brothers would go back, and leave poor Benjamin to be a slave.

Judah then came nearer to Joseph, and began to beg for Benjamin with all his heart.

I promised my father that I would take care of Benjamin. I cannot go home without him. If I were to go back without Benjamin, we should see our father die. Let me be your slave instead of Benjamin, and let him go home to his father; for I could not bear to see my father die of grief.

Now Joseph saw that Judah did indeed love Benjamin and his old father.

Joseph felt ready to burst into tears, yet he did not go out of the room to weep as he had done before; but he said to all his servants, Go out of the room; and Joseph was left alone with his brothers. He cried so loud, that all his servants heard him, though they were not in the room.

At last he said: I am Joseph. Thy brother whom ye sold into Egypt. Is my father yet alive?

Joseph's brothers were frightened; they could not speak, and they dared not come near him.

Joseph did not wish to frighten them; he longed to put his arms round them, and kiss them.

He saw that they were unhappy at the thoughts of their wickedness, so he tried to comfort them.

Do not grieve because you sold me, said he. God let you do it, that I might save corn to feed your children. I wish you all to come and live with me here. You must bring my old father with you, and your children, and I will feed you all. Look at me, and you will see that I am indeed your own brother Joseph. It is my mouth that speaks to you. Go and tell my father what fine things I have in Egypt, and bring him here to live with me.

This was the loving way in which Joseph spoke. Then he threw his arms round Benjamin's neck, and wept as he kissed him; and Benjamin wept too upon Joseph's neck. Afterward Joseph kissed all his brothers, and wept as he kissed each; and then his brothers no more felt afraid of him, but began to talk with him. They saw Joseph had quite forgiven them, and that he loved them with all his heart.

CHAPTER XIX.

JOSEPH, OR THE LONG-LOST SON.

The servants were glad to hear that Joseph had found his brothers. Pharaoh the king heard of the brothers being found; and he was glad, for he loved Joseph.

He called Joseph, and said to him: Your brothers must come and live near you, and you must send for your father, and for all the little children. We will give them houses, fields, and gardens, and they shall live together. We must send wagons to bring the little children, their mothers, and your aged father.

You see how kind the king was.

When all the things were ready, Joseph told his brothers to go to Canaan, and to come back quickly. He gave them one piece of advice before they went. Take care, he said, that you do not quarrel by the way.

Old Jacob had been longing to see them. At last they came, and no one was missing.

They told him quickly the joyful news: Joseph is alive; and he is the great ruler that sells corn in the land of Egypt.

No, said he, my son has long been dead.

But we have seen him.

It cannot be true, said Jacob.

Then the brothers told him that Joseph desired them all to come and live with him.

Still, Jacob could not believe them.

Only come and see the wagons he has sent, said they.

So they took their father to see the wagons, and he did believe.

It is enough, said Jacob. Joseph my son is yet alive; I will go and see him.

The brothers told their wives and children that they must leave Canaan, and take a long journey. Jacob was lame and old, he rode in a wagon, but the brothers walked. They took their sheep, cows, goats and camels, and all their things. They had to travel a very long way. No doubt the little children were much pleased, for children are fond of making journeys.

At last they all came into the land of Egypt.

Long before they came to Joseph's house, they saw a fine chariot coming toward them. It was Joseph's. It stopped, and Joseph got out.

Jacob stepped out of his wagon. His hair was gray, his legs were weak, and he could hardly walk. Joseph was a fine and stately man. He ran to meet his father, and threw his arms round his neck; and then he wept.

The last time Joseph had kissed his father was when he was a boy dressed in his pretty coat, and was going to look for his brothers. How many sad days had Jacob spent since that time.

The brothers did not feel envious now, when they saw Jacob and Joseph folded in each other's arms.

Now, said the aged Jacob, let me die, since I have seen your face once more.

Then Joseph said to his father and brothers: I will go and tell Pharaoh that you have come.

So Joseph went to the king, and said: My father and brothers, and their flocks, and all that they have, are come.

And Pharaoh said to them: What is your employment?

We are shepherds.

Pharaoh said that he would give them a great many fields, and that they might live there altogether, with their children and their flocks.

Joseph wished them to live altogether, because the people in Egypt worshiped idols.

Joseph wished the king to see his dear old father; so he brought him in to the king. The king treated him with great respect.

Jacob lifted up his hands over Pharaoh's head, and prayed God to show him kindness. This was called blessing him. Jacob blessed Pharaoh, because he had been good to Joseph, and paid him so many honors.

Pharaoh said to Jacob: How old are you? Jacob said: I am one hundred and thirty years old.

Jacob at last fell sick, and knew that he should die. He sent for his sons, that he might bless them before he died. When his sons came, he sat upon the bed, and called them one by one, that he might give a blessing to each.

Joseph fell upon his father's face, when he was dead, and wept and kissed him.

A very sad thought came into the minds of the brothers: Perhaps Joseph has only been so kind to us to please his father; perhaps he has not really forgiven us; and now perhaps he will punish us. But Joseph said: Fear not: it was wrong in you to sell me, yet God made it turn out for good. I will still feed

JOSEPH, OR THE LONG-LOST SON.

you and your children. He spoke very kindly, and comforted them.

Joseph lived to be a very old man, and at last he died.

You have heard the history of Abraham, Isaac, and Jacob. God loved them all three. Abraham was the grandfather, Isaac the father, and Jacob the son.

God had promised the land of Canaan to the children of Abraham, Isaac, and Jacob; that is, to their descendants. God would not forget that promise.

CHAPTER XX.

MOSES, OR THE BASKET OF BULRUSHES.

You have heard how Joseph and his brothers lived happily in Egypt for a long while. At last they grew old and died, but they left a great many children; and their children had a great many children, till at last there were hundreds and thousands. These people were the grandchildren of Jacob, and his great-grandchildren and their children.

Did you know that Jacob had two names?

His other name was Israel. It was a name that God had given him.

All the sons of Jacob were called the children of Israel, or the children of Jacob, and the grandchildren of Jacob were called by this same name, Children of Israel. There were some men, and some women, and some children, and all of them together were called Children of Israel.

The grown-up people were called Children of Israel.

They did not live in Canaan, you remember; they had left Canaan, because no corn grew there for a long while; they lived in Egypt, and took care of their sheep. While the good king Pharaoh lived they were happy. At last he died, and there was another king of Egypt: he too was called Pharaoh.

This new king knew that the children of Israel had come from a great way off, and he said: There are so many of them, perhaps they may some day fight against me with swords, and kill me and my servants. I will make them work hard, and I will try to kill them with hard work.

THE FINDING OF MOSES.

SHEEP IN THE PASTURES.

So he ordered them to make a great many bricks, and build very high walls. He sent some of his men to make them work hard.

The children of Israel were used to taking care of sheep, and that is a pleasant employment. Shepherds lead their sheep to the green fields, and by the side of the quiet waters, and they sit under the shade of a tree when the sun is hot. But now the children of Israel were obliged to dig up the clay, and to make bricks, and to dry them in the sun; and if they did not make a great number of bricks, the men whom Pharaoh had sent, beat them. So now they were very unhappy: they often sighed and groaned, and shed tears.

Yet all this hard work did not kill them; so the king thought of another plan. He said: Let every boy that is born be thrown into the river. He did not order the girls to be drowned, because they would not be able to fight with swords when they grew up.

Whenever the king heard that one of the children of Israel had a little boy born, he sent his men to throw it into the river.

There was a very good woman, who had a little boy babe; she was one of the children of Israel. This woman knew that God would take care of her child. She hid her babe, so that Pharaoh's men could not find it. I do not know where she put it, but God taught her to hide it in a very safe place.

When the child was three months old, she found that she could not hide him any more. What should she do with him?

You have heard of the great river of Egypt. Close by the river there grew a great many reeds and bulrushes, which are

like very high, thick grass. She took some bulrushes, and made them into a large basket. She wished to make a basket into which the water could not come; so she got some pitch, and covered the basket with pitch. Then she put her little boy inside, and took the basket in her arms. No one could tell what was in the basket.

She went to the river-side, and laid the basket among the great rushes, close by the water. She knew that God would not let the child be killed; and so she left it, trusting in Him.

She had a little girl much older than the babe. This little girl stood a great way off, to see what would become of her little brother. Soon she saw ladies walking by the river-side. One of them was King Pharaoh's daughter. She was a princess. The other ladies were her maids, and they were going with the princess to some place where she could bathe; for Egypt is a very hot country, and people bathe often in hot countries.

The princess was looking at the rushes, when she saw something very strange peeping out among them. When she saw it, she said to one of her maids, Go, and see what that is. So the maid went, and found the basket. She took it up and brought it to the princess. The princess opened the basket, and saw a sweet babe. It was fair and lovely.

It began to weep. Poor infant! it was used to lie in its mother's arms, but now there was no one to feed it or comfort it. The princess pitied the child. She had heard that her father had ordered every man-child to be thrown into the river, and she said: I suppose this is the child of one of the children of Israel. She did not wish it thrown into the river.

MOSES BROUGHT BEFORE PHARAOH'S DAUGHTER.

The babe's sister had come nearer, and saw that the princess pitied it; so she said: If you want a nurse, I could find you one who would nurse the child for you. The princess said: Go.

Whom did she call? The child's mother. When she had come, the princess said to her: Take this child, and nurse it for me, and I will give you wages.

How glad the mother was to take care of it! She saw that God had heard her prayers, and saved her child from being drowned.

The mother could teach him about God as soon as he could understand. But when he was a big child, the princess sent for him to come and live with her, and she called him her son. She gave him a name. I shall call him Moses, she said—which means "drawn out," for he was drawn out of the water.

The princess lived in a fine house, and had many servants. Moses had beautiful clothes, nice things to eat, and servants to wait upon him. He had no hard work to do, yet he was not idle, but learned a great many things. The princess told wise men to teach him.

He knew the names of the stars, the beasts, birds, and plants. He grew very wise. One thing these wise men could not teach him—about God; for they worshiped idols. Yet Moses did know about God, for his father and mother knew the true God, and when he was a child, Moses lived with them. Of all the things Moses knew, this was the best. He was wiser than all the men in Egypt, for he knew the true God.

He was brave as well as wise, and the people in Egypt praised him, and paid him respect.

CHAPTER XXI.

MOSES, OR THE PIOUS CHOICE.

I have told you how the children of Israel worked making bricks. When Moses became a man, he thought, I live in a fine house, and am as great as a prince. I have no work to do; but my poor cousins, the children of Israel, are working like slaves. Cannot I help them? This thought made him very sorrowful.

Do you remember the promise God made to Abraham about his children and children's children? These children of Israel were the descendants of Abraham.

Abraham's child was called Isaac; Abraham's grandchild was Jacob; and Abraham's great-grandchildren were Joseph and his brothers. Now Joseph's children were Abraham's great-great-grandchildren, and their children were his great-great-great-grandchildren. The children of Israel called Abraham their great-great-great-grandfather; only they had never seen him; he died before they were born.

I will tell you about these great-great-grandchildren of Abraham, and Isaac, and Jacob, and about their children, and I shall call them the Children of Israel.

God had said that they should live in the land of Canaan—that fine land, full of hills and rivers, grass and flowers, sheep and cows, milk and honey. God had said to Abraham, I will give this land to your children. Not to Isaac, but to his great-great-great-great-grandchildren.

Moses had heard of this promise; probably his mother told

him. He had heard how he had been saved from being drowned when a little babe, and he believed that God would let him bring the children of Israel into Canaan. He wished to save them from being slaves among the wicked people of Egypt and to make them happy in that pleasant land of Canaan.

ISRAELITES IN BONDAGE IN EGYPT.

Moses left the king's fine house and all his fine things, and went to the place where the poor Israelites were working. The children of Israel were sometimes called Israelites.

He wished to see whether they remembered God's promise to Abraham, and whether they wished to go to Canaan.

When Moses came to the place the sight he saw was a sad one. They were laboring in the heat of the sun. They worked from morning to night. They dug up the clay to make bricks; that was hard work. When they made the bricks, they put them in heaps to dry in the sun. Then they carried them to

MOSES SMITING THE EGYPTIAN.

build the great walls for Pharaoh, which was very hard labor for these poor men.

They were forced to make a great many bricks. They groaned and cried, but still they were made to do their tasks.

For the men set them a task; not such a little task as you

have, but a great task. The men said: You must make so many bricks.

One day he saw one of the task-masters beating one of the children of Israel. Moses could not bear to see the poor slaves treated so cruelly. Moses looked to see whether there were any more task-masters near: he saw no one. So he killed the task-master, and then dug a hole in the ground, and covered his body over with the earth.

Do you think it was wrong in Moses to kill the task-master? It is very wicked to kill people, for God has commanded people not to kill each other.

But Moses had been sent by God to kill this wicked man, that he might show the Israelites that he had come from God to make them happy. So it was *not* wrong in Moses to kill the man, because God had sent him to do it.

One of the Israelites saw him, and soon King Pharaoh heard of it, and Pharaoh was very angry, and tried to find Moses, that he might punish him. So Moses was obliged to go into a country a great way off, where the king could not find him. God loved Moses, and took care of him wherever he went.

Moses might have lived always in a fine house, and ridden in a chariot, and had many servants; but you see how much he loved the children of Israel.

CHAPTER XXII.

MOSES, OR THE BURNING BUSH.

Moses was grieved to have the poor children of Israel groaning in Egypt; but he was forced to hide himself from Pharaoh. He took nothing with him on his journey—no servant or companion.

At last Moses came to a place where there was grass, and a great many sheep. Here, also, there was a well, and he sat down by the side of it; for he had taken a long journey. He had no house, no bed, and no friends.

Soon there came seven girls to the well. They were sisters, and took care of their father's sheep. They brought their sheep to give them water. First they let down pails into the well, and then poured the water into troughs that stood near. The sheep drank out of the troughs. While they were doing this, some shepherds came to the well, and tried to drive them away, that their own sheep might drink; but the girls had filled the troughs with water and it would have been unfair to have taken the water from their sheep. But the men were stronger than they were, and often behaved in this way to them.

Moses did not like to see weak people ill-treated, and he was very strong; so he stood up, and would not let the shepherds send the girls away, but helped them to draw water for their sheep.

The poor girls thought that Moses was very kind, because he was only a stranger, and yet he had helped them.

When they went home their father said: How is it that you

MOSES, OR THE BURNING BUSH.

are home so soon to-day? And they said: A stranger was by the well, he helped draw water for our sheep.

Then the father answered: Where is the man? Ask him to come and eat bread with us. So the girls called Moses.

The old father asked Moses to live with him and his

MT. HOREB.

daughters; and Moses said he would. Moses took care of the father's sheep, and married one of the girls. Then the father became Moses' father-in-law.

Moses had once been a fine prince, and had ridden in a chariot; but now he led his sheep to eat grass among the green hills.

MOSES, OR THE BURNING BUSH.

There was one thing that must have made Moses sad. He knew that the children of Israel were still groaning at their hard work. King Pharaoh had died; but there was another king Pharaoh as wicked as he had been.

At last the children of Israel cried earnestly to God to help

MOSES AND THE BURNING BUSH.

them, and God heard their prayers, and He determined to save them.

I presume you have all heard of Mt. Horeb.

One day Moses was with the sheep among these high hills. He was quite alone. He looked up, and saw a bush on fire. He saw the bush was still burning, but did not burn up. This surprised him very much, and he said: I will go and look at the bush, and see why it is not burnt up.

He was just going up to it, when he heard some one speaking. The voice came out of the bush. It was the voice of God, who said to him: Moses, Moses!

He answered: Here am I.

Then God said: Come not near this place, for I am here. I have heard the children of Israel crying, and I remember that I promised Abraham that his children should live in Canaan, and I am going to send them there. Moses, you must go to Pharaoh, and tell him to let them go.

This was a hard thing for Moses to do, but God said: I will be with you, and help you.

Then Moses said: But perhaps the children of Israel will not choose to come out of Egypt. They will say: We will not go with you, Moses; you are not speaking the truth. What shall I do then?

God said that He would teach him to do wonderful things. God said: What do you hold in your hand?

Now Moses had a long stick in his hand, called a rod. He used to help his sheep to get out of holes with his rod, and when he climbed high hills, he leaned upon it. So when God said, What do you hold in your hand? Moses answered, A rod.

Throw it upon the ground, said the Lord. And Moses did, and it was turned into a serpent. Moses was afraid of the serpent, and began to run away.

Then God said: Take hold of it by the tail. So Moses **took** hold of it, and it was turned again into a rod.

God said to Moses: When you go to Egypt, do this wonderful thing before the children of Israel, to show them that I have sent you: but if they will not believe you, do this thing too, that I will show you. Put your hand into your bosom.

So Moses put in his hand, and then he drew it out, and it was leprous, that is, it was all covered over with white spots. What a frightful sight.

Then God said: Put your hand in again; and he put it in, and pulled it out again, and then it was as well as before.

Then God said to Moses: If the children of Israel will not believe I have really spoken to you, let them see you do this wonder.

But, said Moses, I do not know what words to say. Then God told Moses that Aaron, his brother, should go with him and speak for him. You have not heard of Aaron before. He could speak well, he was a good man, and loved God. So God was willing that he should help his brother.

Moses went back to his father-in-law, and told him that he must go back to Egypt; and he took his wife and his two little sons with him.

As Moses was going to Egypt, he met his brother Aaron, who was glad to see him, and kissed him. Then Moses and Aaron went together to the land of Egypt.

They found the poor Israelites at their hard work. Aaron said to them, God has sent us to tell Pharaoh to let you go to the land of Canaan. Then Aaron did the wonders that God had shown Moses when He spoke to him from the bush.

The people of Israel believed what Aaron said. They

wished to go the land of Canaan, and they thanked God for having heard their prayers.

They said, We will go; and they bowed their heads, and thanked the Lord for his goodness.

But Moses could not take them out of Egypt till Pharaoh had given him leave.

PYRAMIDS OF EGYPT.

CHAPTER XXIII

MOSES, OR THE FIRST PLAGUES

The next day Moses and Aaron, and some of the children of Israel, went in to speak to King Pharaoh. He was a proud and wicked man who worshiped idols.

Do you think Pharaoh let them go? No; he said: Who is the Lord, that I should obey His voice?

He was now more unkind than before to the children of Israel, and ordered the taskmasters to make them work harder.

As Moses and Aaron came out from king Pharaoh, they saw some of the children of Israel waiting for them. They said: You have done us harm by asking Pharaoh to let us go. He makes us work harder than ever.

It was ungrateful to speak in this manner to Moses, who had tried to help them. But he was very meek and gentle, and he did not answer angrily, but went and prayed to God.

God told him to go to king Pharaoh, and show him the wonder of the serpent. So Moses said to Aaron: Take this rod and throw it on the ground. Aaron did so, and it became a live serpent; then afterward turned into a rod again.

Would Pharaoh now say he would let Israel go? No, he would not; his heart was very hard.

So God told Moses to do another wonderful thing.

Moses and Aaron went early in the morning down to the side of the river, and waited there till Pharaoh came to bathe. Then they said to him: Because you would not do as God desired, and let Israel go, now you shall see what God can do.

Then Aaron took the rod, and lifted it up over the waters; and in a moment, the water was turned into blood.

AARON CAST DOWN THE ROD.

When Pharaoh saw this wonder, he turned back, and went into his house, and would not obey God.

The people of Egypt had nothing to drink, for all the water n the ponds was turned into blood, and all the water in jugs, and basins, and cups, was turned into blood. The fish in the

.iver died. The water was blood for a whole week, and could not be used.

As Pharaoh would not mind, God sent him another plague.

Aaron stretched out the rod, and thousands and thousands of frogs came hopping out of the river, and out of the ponds. They went into the streets, into the houses, into the bedrooms, and into the beds; they went into kitchens, and got among the food; they even went into Pharaoh's house, and into his bed.

Then Pharaoh called for Moses and Aaron, and said to them, Pray God to take away the frogs. I will tell the children of Israel to go.

Moses went and prayed to God, and God made all the frogs die; but then Pharaoh said: I will not let the people go.

So God sent another plague.

Aaron stretched out the rod, and turned all the dust into vile little insects, that crawled over men and over beasts; but Pharaoh would not mind this plague.

Then God sent swarms of flies, that came in at the windows, in doors and out of doors. But no flies came near the children of Israel.

Then Pharaoh said: I will let you go, if God will take away the flies. Then Moses prayed, and God took the flies away. Then Pharaoh said again: I will not let the people go.

So another plague was sent.

The beasts fell very sick—the horses, camels, cows, and the sheep—and many of them died. Yet Pharaoh would not let the people go.

Afterward God made a great many boils come on all the men and women and children; but not upon the children of

Israel. They were so sick they could not stand; yet Pharaoh would not mind, for his heart grew harder and harder.

I have now told you of six plagues. Try and remember what they were.

1. Water turned into blood. 2. Frogs. 3. Small insects. 4. Flies. 5. Death of the beasts. 6. Boils.

I shall soon tell you of some more plagues that God sent to Pharaoh.

God was much stronger than Pharaoh, and was able to make him do what He commanded, and it was very foolish in Pharaoh not to mind God.

CHAPTER XXIV.

MOSES, OR THE LAST PLAGUES.

One morning Moses and Aaron went to Pharaoh, and said: To-morrow God is going to rain great hail-stones, such hail-stones as were never seen in Egypt before. They will kill all men and beasts that are out of doors.

A great many of the men of Egypt heard Moses and Aaron say this. Some of them believed their words. They kept their beasts in their stables, and told their servants to keep in doors. But some did not believe, and let their beasts remain in the field.

The next day Moses stretched out his rod, and God sent thunder, hail, and fire, which ran along the ground. It was a dreadful storm—such a storm as was never seen before. The noise of the hail-stones, and thunder, made every one tremble. But how glad those must have been who were in their houses. Many beasts and men were killed, the grass and corn were burned up by the fire, and the trees were broken. Yet there was no hail where the children of Israel were.

This storm frightened Pharaoh, and he sent for Moses and Aaron, and said: I have sinned; pray the Lord to send no more thunder and hail, and I will let the children of Israel go.

Moses said: I will stretch out my hands to God, and He will not send any more thunder and hail; but still I know you will not obey God.

Then Moses stretched out his hands, and God made the hail and thunder stop, and the rain leave off.

When Pharaoh saw that the storm was over, he would not let the children of Israel go.

Then Moses and Aaron went to king Pharaoh again, and said: God will now send locusts into your country.

Locusts are insects about the size of a child's thumb. Thousands of them fly close together in the air, and they perch upon the trees, and eat up the leaves and fruit.

Moses stretched out the rod, and God made the wind blow hard, and next day the wind blew locusts into Egypt. The locusts made the sky look black, as the wind blew them along; but they did not stay in the air: they perched on the trees, and ate all the fruit that the hail had left; they covered the grass and ate it up, and they even came into the houses.

Pharaoh and his servants thought that they should soon have nothing to eat. Pharaoh sent quickly for Moses and Aaron. I have sinned, he said. Only forgive me this once, and pray God to take away the locusts, and I will let Israel go.

So Moses prayed to the Lord. God sent another wind, and it blew the locusts away.

But Pharaoh still said: I will not let Israel go.

How sad it must have been to have walked in the fields after the locusts had been there. It was the pleasant spring, but it looked like winter. There were no leaves on the trees, there was no tender grass; all was bare as in winter. What misery Pharaoh's wickedness had brought upon the land!

The next time Moses did not tell Pharaoh what God was going to do. Moses stretched out his rod toward heaven, and in a moment God made it darker than ever it is at night, except where the children of Israel lived; there it was light.

MOSES, OR THE LAST PLAGUES.

The people of Egypt were frightened. They were doing their work, or eating, or walking, when all at once this darkness came on. They sat down and never moved, night nor day. Now they had time to think of all their wickedness.

It was dark three days and three nights, and then it grew light.

But was Pharaoh sorry for his wickedness? No; his heart was harder than ever. He said to Moses, Get away; you shall never see my face again.

God spoke to Moses again, and said: I am going to send another plague. At night I shall come into every house in Egypt, and kill the eldest son of every person. But this is what I desire the children of Israel to do. Let each man take a lamb, a lamb without spot, and kill it,

EGYPTIAN DOORWAY.

and eat it to-night with his family: and let him take the blood of the lamb, and put the blood outside the door, and when I pass I shall see the blood, and I will not kill the eldest son in that house. Let the people in the house stand round the table while they eat the lamb. Let them all be dressed ready for a journey.

So all the children of Israel killed young lambs, roasted them, and ate them at night. They stood around their tables with their walking sticks in their hands. They ate bread with the lamb, and bitter herbs. They put blood on the posts of the door, for then they knew they were safe.

The men of Egypt went to bed that night as usual, but in the middle of the night the eldest son in each house died. No one saw God's angel enter in, but yet he came. No bars nor

DEATH OF THE FIRST-BORN.

bolts could keep him out; but when he saw the blood on a door, then he passed over that house.

What a dreadful cry the fathers and mothers made in Egypt when they found their eldest sons were dead! They rushed out of their houses weeping. Our darling son is dead! said one. And so is mine! said another. And mine! And mine! There never was such dreadful lamenting heard in Egypt before.

Even Pharaoh's eldest son was killed, as well as the sons of poor people. Pharaoh rose up at night, and called for Moses and Aaron, but it was dark, so that they did not see his face.

Go, said Pharaoh, and take the children of Israel with you; they may take their sheep and cows with them, and all that they have.

The men of Egypt begged them to go as fast as possible, for they were afraid that God would kill them all.

Then the Israelites said to the women of Egypt, Give us some gold and silver before we go.

And they said: We will give you whatever you want; only go.

The Israelites had done a great deal of work in Egypt, and it was right they should have some money for it.

So they gave them a great many beautiful things.

The Israelites went away in a great hurry. They took their things just as they were. They put bread in their bags —they drove their sheep, cows, and camels, and asses, before them, and set out in the night.

There was a great crowd of people. More people than live in any great town, except London. No little child could have counted them.

So at last they came out of Egypt, where they had been slaves so long. God had remembered His promise to Abraham.

God said to Moses: They must never forget my kindness

in bringing them out of Egypt. They must eat a lamb every year, as they have done to-night. Eating the lamb shall be called eating the Passover. This supper was called the Feast of the Passover, because God passed over the doors where the blood was seen.

EGYPTIAN ASSES.

CHAPTER XXV.

MOSES, OR THE RED SEA.

The children of Israel had begun their journey to Canaan; they had to travel a long way before they could reach that pleasant place.

God showed them the way. He went before them in a dark cloud. The cloud moved, and they moved after it. But a black cloud could not be seen at night, so at night God made the cloud shine like fire. When the cloud or the fire stopped, then Moses desired all the people to set up their tents on the ground.

As soon as the cloud moved, the people folded up their tents, placed them on the backs of their camels, and went on their journey.

The children of Israel went very fast till they came to the seaside. Then the cloud stopped, and they set up their tents close by the sea. This sea was called the Red Sea; the water was like other water, though it was called the Red Sea.

They had not been long in their tents, before they heard a great noise of wheels and horses. They looked, and saw a great way off, Pharaoh and a host of soldiers in chariots, and on horses. Pharaoh had been sorry that he had let them go.

The Israelites were frightened. They could not get over the sea, for they had no ships; yet, if they staid where they were, Pharaoh and his men would soon overtake them. What could they do? They cried to God to help them. This was right; but they did something else that was not right, they began to speak angrily to Moses.

It was ungrateful, but he answered them meekly: Do not be afraid; God will fight for you, and you shall never see the faces of Pharaoh and his men again.

Then Moses prayed to God; for Moses knew that God would save them.

God said to Moses: Lift up your rod over the sea, and I will make a dry path for the Israelites to walk upon.

VIEW ON THE RED SEA.

So Moses lifted up his rod, and the waters obeyed him; and part of the waters were lifted up on one side, and part on the other, and seemed like two walls of water, while a dry path was seen between.

The Israelites walked in the path, and all their cattle with them. It was the evening when they began to cross the sea, and they were walking across all the night; yet it was not dark, because the cloud in the sky shone brightly in the night, and gave light; God did not choose that Pharaoh should see the light; so God made the bright cloud move backward, and it stood in the sky between the Israelites and Pharaoh: the bright side was turned toward the Israelites, and the dark side toward Pharaoh, so the Israelites saw a bright light. The hosts of Pharaoh were in the dark, and they could not go fast because it was dark; but the Israelites walked quickly along

CROSSING THE RED SEA.

the dry path, and by the morning they got to the land that was on the other side of the sea. They had not yet got to Canaan, but they had got over the sea, and were on their journey to Canaan.

When Pharaoh and his men came to the edge of the sea, they saw a dry path through the sea, and the walls of water on each side; so they went along the dry path. When they had gone about half way across the sea, and were hoping soon to overtake the Israelites, God looked at them. Pharaoh and his men heard dreadful noises, and they were very much frightened.

They could not make their chariots go on, and they thought that God was going to help the Israelites to kill them; so they said to each other, Let us turn back.

But it was now too late; God was going to destroy those wicked men: they drove as fast as they could, that they might get out of the water, but it was too late; for the walls of water fell down and covered them all, and they were drowned in the midst of the sea.

This was the end of Pharaoh and his wicked servants. As soon as the Israelites got over, God desired Moses to lift up his rod, and let the walls of water fall down and cover the dry path. Moses had done as God told him; and Pharaoh and his men, who were in the middle of the sea, had been drowned.

Now the Israelites saw that the cruel men could hurt them no more. God had punished them for their wickedness, and had saved the poor children of Abraham as He had promised.

This was a happy morning for the Israelites. They thanked

MIRIAM AND HER MAIDENS.

God for His goodness, and they sung together a beautiful song of praise.

Miriam, the prophetess, took a timbrel in her hand, and with all the others rejoiced.

How pleasant it must have been to see the Israelites singing and rejoicing. A little while before, they had been working hard in the sun, now they were on their way to a good land, where they might live happily.

JOSEPH'S DREAM.

CHAPTER XXVI.

MOSES, OR THE MANNA AND THE ROCK.

The children of Israel were very glad to get away from their cruel masters. Now they had no hard work to do, and they had a kind master. Ought they not to be good and happy?

They were now in a very large wilderness. There were no men nor houses in this wilderness, but there were lions and bears, who roared and howled; there were serpents that bite, and scorpions that sting; there were no rivers nor brooks, but there were high hills, and dark pits. There were scarcely any fruit-trees or corn-fields, so that there was very little to eat; and the Israelites could not sow grain, nor plant fruit-trees, because they were traveling.

There was such a number of people that they wanted a great deal of food to feed them. They had taken but little bread with them in their bags, when they left Egypt, and soon they ate it up.

God loved them, and would not let them starve. Still these ungrateful Israelites murmured. They went to Moses and Aaron, and said: We wish we had died in Egypt. At least, we there had bread and meat, as much as we could eat; but now we shall be starved.

How ungrateful they still were to Moses and to God.

Moses did not answer roughly. He knew that God heard their wicked words; and God called to Moses, and said: I have heard them, and I will feed them.

Next morning, when they looked out at their tent-doors, they saw the ground was white. They looked to see what made the ground white, and saw little round white things on the ground. They said to each other: What can this be? We never saw anything like it before.

Then Moses said: This is the bread that God has sent you from heaven; gather it, and take it to your tents.

So all the men got jugs, and baskets, and gathered the manna for themselves, for their wives, and for their little children; and there was enough for them all. They tasted it, and found it was as sweet as honey, and they called it "manna."

Then they took it home, and their wives cooked it for dinner; they crumbled it, and baked it, and made it into cakes. They had manna for breakfast, for dinner, and for supper; nothing but manna. It was very nice and wholesome. It was more fit for angels than for men to eat, because it came from heaven, and did not grow out of the ground as corn does. God sent it very early, before it was light, and every one was obliged to get up early to gather it, because, when the sun was hot, it melted away; so that if the Israelites did not get up soon, they had no food.

Moses said to them: Do not save any of the manna, for God will send you some every day. If it is all gone at night, do not be afraid; trust God. He will send you more.

But some of the people chose to save some of the manna. They were disobedient. They looked at their manna next morning, but it was full of worms. They could not eat it, but threw it away.

MOSES ON THE MOUNT.

Soon afterward the people had no water to drink. There was no river in the wilderness, and very few wells or ponds.

These unbelieving Israelites thought God would let them die of thirst. So they went to Moses, and spoke very angrily.

Why did you bring us up out of Egypt? You mean to kill us, and our little children, and our cattle with thirst.

They were very angry. Moses did not answer, but began to pray to God: What shall I do for these people?

Then God said to Moses: Take your rod, and go up a hill, and let some of the people go with you. Then, when you are come to a high place, close by a rock, strike the rock, and water shall come out.

So Moses took some people with him, and struck the rock, and water came running out.

The people at the bottom of the hill saw water running down like a river, and flowing upon the dry ground.

What a pleasant sight for the thirsty people! Their mouths were dry, and their tongues were stiff, their throats burning, but now they might stoop down and drink, or they might fill their jugs with water. The poor cows, and sheep and horses ran to the water to drink.

CHAPTER XXVII.

MOSES, OR MOUNT SINAI.

The Israelites went on through the wilderness, which was very large, and it would be a long while before they could get to Canaan.

They soon came to a very high mountain, called Mount Sinai. It was the same mountain where Moses had seen the bush on fire when he was keeping his sheep. Now he had brought the children of Israel to that very place where God first had spoken to him.

The Israelites placed their tents near the bottom of the mountain; for the cloud had stopped, and so the Israelites knew that they were to wait in that place.

God told Moses to come up to the top of the mountain, for he had something to say to him. So Moses went up. Then God said to him: You see how kind I have been to the children of Israel in bringing them out of Egypt; go down and ask them whether they will do what I command them; if they will, they shall always be my people.

So Moses went down and asked them if they would obey God. And they said: Yes, we will do all that the Lord tells us.

Then Moses went up to the top of the mountain again, and told God the people would do all that He commanded.

Then God said: I am going to let the people hear my voice, and they shall see me speaking to you. Go down and tell them to get ready.

So Moses went down and said: In three days you will

hear God's voice, and see him in a cloud at the top of the mountain. Get ready.

So the people washed their clothes, that they might all stand in clean white clothes before the Lord. Moses desired men to put rails all round the mount, that no one might go up the mount, or even touch it; even the sheep must not eat the grass, for it was the mount of God.

IN THE WILDERNESS OF SINAI.

In three days, early in the morning, the people heard a loud voice, and they all trembled. Moses desired them to come out of their tents, and to look upon God.

What a dreadful sight they saw. The mountain was shaking and moving up and down. On the top a great fire was seen, and a thick cloud, and such a smoke went up as filled the sky with blackness. There were thunders and lightnings, and a sound came out of the fire like the sound of a trumpet, and every moment it grew louder and louder. Even Moses himself was frightened, and said: I tremble, and am afraid.

The Lord said to Moses: Come up to me on the top of the mount.

So Moses went up, and all the people saw him go. He

went upon the shaking mount, and into the midst of the smoke.

When Moses came up, God said to him: Go tell the people not to come up after you, for they must not come up this mountain.

And Moses said: I have put rails round the mount.

But still God said: Go and tell them not to come near; for God knew how bold and disobedient the people were.

So Moses went down and said: Do not dare to touch the mountain.

Then God spoke very loud indeed, so that all the people heard; and as they heard they trembled.

These are, in substance, God's words: I am the Lord, thy God, that brought thee out of the land of Egypt.

I. Thou shalt have no other gods before me.

II. Thou shalt not make images, and worship them.

III. Thou shalt not take the name of the Lord, thy God, in vain.

IV. Remember the Sabbath day to keep it holy.

V. Honor thy father and thy mother.

VI. Thou shalt not kill.

VII. Thou shalt not commit adultery.

VIII. Thou shalt not steal.

IX. Thou shalt not bear false witness against thy neighbor.

X. Thou shalt not covet.

God said this on the mount, and then He said no more.

The people were glad when God had left off speaking, for they could not bear the sound of that terrible voice; but while He was speaking, they had gone farther and farther away.

Soon they came to Moses, and they said to him: Ask God never to let us hear His voice again, it frightens us so much. We wish God to tell everything to you, and you can tell us what He says.

MOSES GIVING THE PEOPLE THE COMMANDMENTS.

So Moses went up again to the dark cloud at the top of the mount, and told God what the people had said. They do not wish to hear Thee speak to them again, said Moses.

And God said: They have done well in not wishing to hear my voice. I shall speak to you, and you shall tell them; and oh! that they would obey me, and that I might bless them always. God told Moses to come up to Him quite alone, and to stay with Him at the top of the mountain; and so Moses staid with God forty days and forty nights, and all that time he neither ate bread nor drank water; but God kept him alive, and talked to him out of the thick cloud.

At the end of the time, God gave Moses a book. It was not made of paper, like the books you have seen, but it was made of stone. It had only two leaves, and on those leaves very little writing. God had written in it with His own finger.

You would like to know what was written in it. God had written in it all the words He had spoken in the loud voice from the cloud. The ten things God had told the Israelites, are called the ten commandments.

He had written them down that Moses might read them to the children of Israel, so that they might never forget God's commandments.

CHAPTER XXVIII.

MOSES, OR THE GOLDEN CALF.

While Moses staid in the mount, at first the Israelites behaved well, but at last they grew tired of waiting. They wanted to go on to Canaan quickly, but the cloud stopped at the top of the mountain, and they were not allowed to go on unless it moved. Moses was on the top of the mountain and they began to think he would never come back; so they went to Aaron, and said: Make us some gods to go before us, for we do not know what is become of Moses.

This was a wicked thing to ask, but you know they had lived in Egypt, where they had seen people worship idols, and they had learned to do the same.

Aaron was afraid that they would kill him if he did not make an image that would please them, so he said: Bring me your gold ear-rings. And the people did so.

The women of Egypt had given them gold before they set out on their journey.

Aaron melted all the ear-rings in the fire, then, when the gold was soft, he formed it into an image. He made it in the shape of a calf. The people in Egypt worshiped calves, and so he chose that animal for them to worship.

As soon as the Israelites saw it they began to praise it, and say: This is he who brought us out of Egypt. Then Aaron put it on a high place, and built an altar before it, and said that they would have a great feast the next day.

The next day they rose up early. They spent the day in

worshiping the calf. They took their lambs and goats, and offered them on the altar, and then rose up to sing.

You remember that they had promised a little while ago always to obey God; but they did not keep their promise. One

WORSHIPING THE CALF.

of the ten commandments was: Thou shalt not make an image and bow down to it. How soon they broke that commandment!

Moses was at the top of the mountain talking with God.

He did not know what they were doing, but God knew, and He said to Moses: Go down; the people you brought out of Egypt have made a golden calf, and are worshiping it. I am very angry with them, and I will kill them all; but I will save you and your children.

MOSES BREAKING THE TABLES OF STONE.

Moses was grieved to hear that the Lord was angry, and he entreated God to forgive the people. Remember, he said, how you brought them out of Egypt, and how you promised Abraham that you would bless his children. And the Lord heard Moses' prayer; and determined that He would not kill them all.

MOSES, OR THE GOLDEN CALF.

Then Moses went quickly down the mount, with the book of stone in his hand. When he had almost come to the bottom he heard the noise of singing, and he knew that it was the Israelites praising their calf. At last he came to the tents, and he saw the calf, and the people dancing round it, like mad or

MOSES DESTROYING THE IDOLS.

drunken people. It was a dreadful sight for Moses to see. He grew more angry still, and he threw down the stone book upon the ground, and broke it into pieces. The Israelites had broken God's law, and Moses broke the book in his grief. Moses would not give that stone book to these wicked people.

They had thought they should never see Moses again, but he had caught them in their wickedness.

He took the calf, no one trying to hinder him, and threw it again into the fire; then afterward ground it into powder, and

MOSES AND AARON.

threw it into some water, and made the Israelites drink that bitter water.

Moses was very angry with Aaron for having made the calf. Moses said to him: Why did you let the people be so wicked?

Aaron said: Do not be angry with me; the people chose to be wicked, and they asked me to make the calf; I did it to please them.

You have heard how the stone book was broken. God did not make a new one Himself, but He called Moses up into the mountain again, and then God wrote the ten commandments in a new book of stone, which he told Moses to make. God talked to Moses as friends talk to one another. He did not speak in that loud voice which had frightened the Israelites. Moses liked being with God upon the mountain. God let Moses see some of His glorious brightness; but God would not let him see His face. The angels in heaven see God's face, but men upon earth could not bear such brightness.

Moses ate no bread, and drank no water when he was alone with God.

At last Moses came down again to the people, with the stone book in his hand. This time the Israelites were not worshiping an image; they came up to Moses to speak to him; but when they looked at his face, they were afraid to come near him; even Aaron, Moses' brother, was afraid.

The reason was, Moses' face shone like the sun, and they could not bear such brightness.

He had been talking with God and looking upon his glory, and this had made his face so bright. For God is brighter than the sun, and the angels who look upon God are bright like him.

When Moses knew why the people could not come near him, he took a thick veil, and covered his face, for he wanted to tell them what God had said.

Then Aaron and the people came to him.

CHAPTER XXIX.

MOSES, OR THE TABERNACLE.

Moses had been with God upon the mount a great many days. God was showing him how to make a beautiful house, which was to be "the house of God." God did not need a house, for His throne is in the sky.

Then Moses called the people and said: First, God commands you to do no work on the Sabbath day, but to worship Him; and He is going to have a beautiful house made, where you can come and pray to Him. Who will bring me things with which to make the house?

You remember that the women of Egypt had given them a great deal of gold, and silver, and cloth, and linen. They had made a calf with some of their gold, but they had a great deal more besides.

But do you think they would give these things to God? Or would they say: We cannot spare our things; we mean to make fine clothes, and to make our tents look pretty inside. Do you think they would part with their pretty things? Yes, they would. They all went into their tents, after Moses had spoken to them. They opened their boxes and their baskets, and they took out gold and silver rings and ear-rings, and they took out beautiful pieces of cloth; some were blue, some were purple, and some were scarlet; and a great deal of fine white linen, and skins of sheep and goats, and beautiful kinds of wood. They brought all these things to Moses.

Some of the rich men had beautiful shining stones, and

sweet spices, and oil; and they brought them all to Moses as gifts toward building a house for the worship of God.

Moses was pleased to see that the people would give their things to God, and most of all he was glad that they liked to give them. If we feel sorry when we give things, God is not pleased.

Moses called the children of Israel, and said: God has made two of you very skillful in cutting stones, in carving wood, and in making all kinds of curious things, and He has told me their names.

Then Moses called these two men, and gave them all the beautiful things, and said: Now begin to make the house, and I shall tell you what you shall make. And Moses called every one to help them; and he told the two skillful men to teach the others.

So all the people began to work. The women spun blue, and purple, and scarlet thread and worsted. The men made the thread into linen and cloth; they cut the wood with saws and hammers; they melted the gold and silver in the fire, and then made altars, candlesticks, shovels, tongs, basins, and many other things. They worked hard for many months till all the things were finished.

I will now tell you what sort of a house God had told Moses to make, and you will soon see how well he obeyed this command of God.

It was not made of bricks nor stone, because this house was to be moved from one place to another; so it was not fastened to the ground, but was made like a tent, and could be moved easily.

You never saw so large a tent as this was. It was as big as a very large room. It was called the Tabernacle.

A great many boards were placed upright on the ground, and close together. These boards were the walls of the house: but there were no boards at the top; curtains were thrown over the house to cover the top. There was no door to the house, but a curtain hung down in front, and that curtain was used instead of a door.

There was no floor to the house: green grass was the only floor.

The house was very beautiful; for the boards were covered with gold, and the curtains were blue, purple, and scarlet, and there were five posts of gold in front, over which a curtain hung down for the door.

The house had two rooms inside. The first room was the largest.

In this room there were three very beautiful things:

1. In the middle an altar of gold; but no lamps were burned upon it, only sweet spices, which gave the tabernacle a very sweet smell. The burning spices were called "incense."

2. On one side there was a golden table, and on the table twelve loaves. They were called the shew-bread, or holy bread. There was fresh bread put there every Sabbath day.

3. On the other side there was a golden candlestick with seven lamps. There was no window in the tabernacle, but these lamps made it light.

This room was very beautiful, but there was another room still more beautiful.

It was the inner room, on the other side of the curtain.

There was a curtain between the large and the small room. This curtain was instead of a door. It was called The Veil.

In the little room there was a golden box, with golden angels on the top. This box was called The Ark. Inside the box the book of stone was placed. But what made this room so glorious was, that God used to come down in His cloud, and fill this small room with His brightness.

The cloud rested between the golden cherubims, or angels, on the top of the box.

The top of the box was called the mercy-seat, because God sat there, and God is full of love and mercy. This little room was called The Holy of Holies.

It had no window in it, and no candle, but yet it was light. The glory of God made it light, for God, you know, is brighter than the sun.

CHAPTER XXX.

MOSES, OR THE PRIESTS.

I have told you what kind of a place the tabernacle was. I am now going to tell you of some things that were placed outside of it. Houses often have a garden round them. The tabernacle had no garden round it, but there was a large piece of ground near it, called The Court; and there were posts round the court. These posts were placed at a little distance from each other, and curtains were hung between the posts; so there was a wall of curtains round the tabernacle.

In this court there were two things, of which I shall speak:
1. A brass altar.

This altar was very large. It was not like the little altar of gold inside the tabernacle. This altar was not for the burning of spices, but for the bnrning of beasts, such as sheep, goats, and calves. You know that God had told people to offer beasts to Him as sacrifices.

This brass altar was for the sacrifices.

2. A brass basin was placed in the court. It was very large, and was filled with water for people to wash in.

God said that Aaron should be high-priest. Aaron was to offer the sacrifices, to burn the incense, and to light the lights in the candlestick.

God said that Aaron might go into the little room, the Holy of Holies; God would not allow any person but Aaron to go in there, and he only allowed him to go in once every year. Aaron might lift up the veil, and see the cloud upon the mercy-seat.

Moses might go in as well as Aaron; and God promised to speak to him in that little room.

God told Moses to have some beautiful clothes made for

A HIGH-PRIEST.

Aaron to wear. The two skillful men of whom I told you before, knew how to make them.

1. He was to wear a white dress with long sleeves.
2. A robe of blue. He was to wear this over the white

dress. Little golden bells were hung round the edge of it; and they would sound sweetly as Aaron moved along.

3. An ephod made of white linen, worked all over with purple, scarlet, and gold. Aaron was to wear the ephod over the blue robe.

4. A band round his waist called a girdle. It was made of white linen, and was worked with purple, scarlet thread, and with gold wire.

5. A breastplate. Aaron was to wear this in front. It was made of linen, covered with twelve shining stones. It was to be fastened to Aaron's shoulders by gold chains..

6. Aaron was to wear a high white cap upon his head, called a mitre. A piece of gold was on the mitre, and on the gold was written, Holiness to the Lord. Aaron ought to be holy, because he was to offer sacrifices to God.

He was to wear no shoes upon his feet; but was often to wash his feet and his hands in the brass basin.

Aaron had four sons. God said that they should help him to offer sacrifices. Aaron's sons were to wear white clothes, but not the same beautiful clothes as Aaron. They were to be called Priests, and Aaron was to be called High-priest.

It was a long while before the tabernacle was made. Though the people worked very hard, yet the things were not finished for almost a year.

At last God commanded Moses to set up the tabernacle.

Moses set up the boards for the walls of the tabernacle, and covered the top with curtains; and he placed the ark in the Holy of Holies; and he put the table, and the candlestick, and the golden altar in the largest room; and he set up the posts,

MOSES, OR THE PRIESTS.

and the curtains, all round the court; and he put the brass altar and basin in it. Then Moses poured sweet oil upon all the things; pouring this oil was called "anointing."

Then Moses put upon Aaron his beautiful clothes, and put the white clothes upon Aaron's sons; and he poured sweet oil upon their heads and anointed them.

Then God came down in His cloud, and His brightness filled the whole place.

CHAPTER XXXI.

MOSES, OR THE ISRAELITES' JOURNEY.

Now the Israelites had a place in which to worship God.

Every morning the priests offered up a lamb on the brass altar, and burned incense on the golden altar in the tabernacle. And every evening they offered another lamb, and burned some more incense.

God sent some fire down from heaven to burn the sacrifices with, and the priests never let the fire go out. Every Sabbath day the priests placed some fresh bread on the golden table, and then took away all the old bread, eating it themselves. **The bread** must be fresh on this table.

While the people had been making the tabernacle, they had staid in one place near the great mount, Sinai; but soon after it was finished, the cloud of God moved. Then the priests blew two silver trumpets, to tell the people that they were to move to another place.

Then the people packed up their tents and furniture, and put them on the backs of their camels, for they were going away, as they were told to do.

Then the priests went into the tabernacle, and covered all the things in it. Then they gave them to men to carry upon their shoulders; but the priests covered the ark with the beautiful veil, and carried it themselves. There were two long golden sticks fastened to it; the priests held the ends of the sticks, and carried it in this way.

Then the priests had men carry the curtains, the posts, **and** the boards of the tabernacle. The priests went first with the ark, and all the people followed them, and God in the cloud showed them the way.

When the cloud stopped, the priests and the people stopped, and set up the tabernacle.

In this manner the Israelites traveled all through the wilderness.

CHAPTER XXXII.

MOSES, OR THE TWELVE SPIES.

At last the Israelites came near the land of Canaan.

They could see the tops of the high hills that were in Canaan, and they wished to know what sort of a land it was, and what sort of people lived in it.

So the Israelites came to Moses and said: We wish to send some men to look at the land; and we wish them to come back and tell us what kind of a land it is.

Moses waited to know whether God would like to have some men go.

Soon God said to Moses: Send twelve men into Canaan to see the land. So Moses called twelve of the children of Israel, and said to them: Go into Canaan, and walk up among the high hills, and look at the land; see whether there are many people there, and what kind of people they are; whether they are strong or weak; see whether there are many trees, and much corn and grass. Bring back some fruit, to show us the kind of fruit that grows.

So the twelve men set out on their journey. These men were called spies. They walked up and down the hills, and by the side of the water. They saw sweet gardens, and fields covered with sheep, and fields full of corn, and trees laden with fruit, and they saw holes in the trees, which the bees had filled with honey, so that honey dropped to the ground. They saw large towns with high walls around them, and they saw many strong men, and some of them were giants.

At last they came to a brook or pond. A vine grew by it, and on the vine there were ripe grapes; one of the bunches was very, very large. They said: Let us carry it back, to show to the children of Israel. One man could not carry this

CARRYING THE GRAPES TO SHOW TO MOSES.

bunch by himself. So they took a staff or stick, and fastened the bunch of grapes to the staff, and one man held one end of the staff, and another held the other. The rest of the men picked figs and other fruit, and carried them back to the tents.

The spies were forty days looking at the land of Canaan.

When they came back, the people saw the beautiful bunch of grapes. There were no such grapes in the wilderness. The spies then said: The land of Canaan is a fine land, full of milk and honey; but we cannot get into it, for the people live in great towns with high walls; they are very strong, and some of them are giants.

Then the children of Israel were frightened, and began to weep.

Ah! said they, we shall be killed if we try to get in.

It was wicked to say this, because God had promised to help them.

Two of the spies were very good men; their names were Joshua and Caleb. They did not wish to frighten the people; and Caleb stood up and said: Let us go into the land, for we can conquer the people that are in it.

But the other ten spies said: No, we cannot; because the people of Canaan are stronger than we.

These ten spies were wicked men, because they knew that God had promised to help the Israelites to conquer the men of Canaan, and they ought to have told the people to trust in God.

The Israelites cried all night long, and said: Oh! that we had died in Egypt, or in the wilderness. The people of Canaan will kill us.

At last they said: Let us go back into Egypt.

They knew that Moses would not take them back, and so they said: We can make another man captain, and he will take us back.

Moses and Aaron heard these wicked words; they were

full of grief and they fell down on the ground upon their faces.

Then Joshua and Caleb stood up and said to the people: We have seen the land, and it is very beautiful; if we trust in God, He will help us. The people of Canaan have no God to help them; therefore we ought not to be afraid of them.

The children of Israel would not listen to Joshua and Caleb, but were going to kill them with stones, when God shone brightly upon the tabernacle, so that the people saw that He was angry.

Moses was lying on his face on the ground, but God spoke to him, and said: How long will this people provoke me?

Then Moses prayed to God for the people.

Oh! pardon this people, he said. Thou hast forgiven them many times.

God heard Moses' prayer, and said: I have pardoned them. They shall not come into Canaan; only their children shall come in. They shall stay in the wilderness forty years, and they shall all die in it; and when their children are grown up, they shall go into the land of Canaan. But there are two of the men who shall go into Canaan; they are Caleb and Joshua.

Moses told the children of Israel what God had said, and when the people heard it, they were very unhappy.

How sad it was for the people to think that they should never see that sweet land of Canaan, but should die in the wilderness. Yet they deserved to die, because they had not believed what God had said.

CHAPTER XXXIII.

MOSES, OR THE SIN OF MOSES AND AARON.

The children of Israel lived in the wilderness a great many years. They moved about from place to place.

At last they came to a place where there was no water

They murmured against Moses and Aaron, as they always did when they were unhappy.

They said: Oh! that we had died before this time! Why did you bring us out of Egypt into this wilderness? Here there are no figs, no grapes, no kind of fruit; and now there is no water to drink.

They forgot that it was because of their own wickedness that they were still in the wilderness; for if they had obeyed God, they would then have been sitting under their own fruit in Canaan.

Moses and Aaron were very much grieved to hear them murmur.

God said: Take the rod and call the people, and go to the rock and *speak* to it, and water shall come out of the rock, and then the people and the beasts shall drink.

So Moses took the rod—the rod was kept near the ark. Then Moses and Aaron called the people together, and told them to look at what they were going to do.

Moses and Aaron felt very angry with the people, and they said: Hear now, ye rebels (which means *murmurers*), must we fetch water for you out of this rock?

Then Moses lifted up his hand and struck the rock twice

with his rod; and the water came flowing out in streams, and the people and the cattle began to drink.

Do you think that Moses and Aaron had behaved right? Had God told them to strike the rock?

God had said: Speak to the rock.

Was it right to speak so impatiently, and to say, Must we fetch water for you, rebels?

Moses and Aaron had been in a passion. God was displeased with them.

God loved Moses and Aaron; yet He would punish them when they did wrong. He would forgive them and take them to heaven, but He would give them some punishment.

Soon after, God said to Moses and Aaron: Because you have done this, you shall not go into Canaan; you shall die in the wilderness.

What a great punishment this was. Moses had often longed to see that good land of Canaan; he had often wished to see the Israelites happy in their own houses and gardens; he had longed to see the place where Abraham had built altars and worshiped God; and now he must die in the wilderness. He prayed to God to spare him this punishment, but God would not. God said: Ask me no more to do this. Then Moses knew that he must bear this punishment.

Moses was the meekest man in all the world. The Israelites had often spoken ungratefully to him, and he had made no answer. Yet at last he himself fell into a passion.

At last the time came for Aaron to die; for God chose that Aaron should die first. God said to Moses: Go up to the top of the hill with Aaron, and take Aaron's eldest son with you;

and Aaron will die on the top, and you must put his clothes upon his son. God chose Aaron's son to be high priest instead of Aaron; so he was to wear Aaron's clothes.

So Aaron put on his beautiful high-priest's clothes; his blue robe with golden bells, and his shining ephod over it, his shining breast-plate, and his white mitre, with the golden writing upon it. Then Aaron walked with Moses and his son to the top of the hill, and all the people looked at them. Aaron knew that he should never walk down the hill, but he obeyed God, and bore his punishment meekly.

When they were come to the top, Moses took the beautiful clothes off his brother Aaron, and put them on Aaron's son.

Moses parted from his brother Aaron on the top of that hill; for there Aaron died. Moses and the son left him dead upon the top, and came down the hill together. Then the people saw that Aaron was dead, and that there was another high-priest.

CHAPTER XXXIV.

MOSES, OR THE SERPENT OF BRASS.

The children of Israel traveled in the wilderness a great many years. Sometimes when they were close to Canaan, the cloud moved the other way, and they were obliged to go on traveling. This made them unhappy, for they longed to get into the happy land of Canaan.

How do you think they bore their punishment? You know they were always ready to murmur. They spoke against God, and against Moses.

God sent them a dreadful punishment this time. You know there were wild beasts and horrible serpents and scorpions in the wilderness; but God took care of the Israelites, so that they were not hurt by them; but now God sent serpents, whose mouths burned like fire. These serpents came rushing among the tents. The Israelites could not get away. If they climbed up a high place, the serpents could climb too, and get through the smallest places.

Many of the Israelites were bitten. After they had been bitten they grew sick, and got worse and worse, till at last they died. There was no medicine that could cure these bites; no plaster would make them well; every person who was bitten was sure to die.

The Israelites came to Moses, and said: We have sinned; we have spoken against the Lord, and against you; pray to the Lord that He take the serpents from us.

Moses was kind and forgiving, and he prayed for the people.

166   MOSES, OR THE SERPENT OF BRASS.

The Lord heard Moses' prayer, and He did more than Moses asked; for God not only called away the serpents, but He told him how to cure the people who were bitten.

He did not tell Moses to give them medicine, or to put a plaster over the bites. He said: Take some brass, and make

THE BRAZEN SERPENT.

it into the image of a serpent, and put it on a pole, and tell the people who are bitten to look at it; and those that look shall be made well.

Moses believed God. He took some brass, and made it

soft in the fire; and then made it like one of the fiery serpents, and put it on a pole, and lifted it up where every one could see it, and called to the sick people to look quickly at the serpent, and be made well.

The people who were bitten could crawl to the doors of their tents, and lift up their dying eyes toward the serpent. After they had looked, their pain went away; they felt well and strong; they could walk and praise God.

VIEW ON THE NILE.

CHAPTER XXXV.

THE DEATH OF MOSES.

The time had almost come for Moses to die. The Israelites were soon to go into Canaan, but Moses was not to go there with them.

Moses had written a great many books; and now he had almost finished them.

He had written about how God made the world, how Adam ate the fruit, how Cain killed Abel. He had written about Noah and Abraham, and Isaac and Jacob; he had written about Joseph and his wicked brethren; he had written about himself, how he had been saved from the water when he was a babe. He had written about the ten plagues and the ten commandments and the tabernacle; he had written about his own sin. All I have told you, Moses had written down in five books; they have all been copied into other books, and we can read all Moses wrote, for it is in the Bible.

Moses did not write in such books as you have seen. His paper was rolled up like a piece of cloth. He wrote five rolls; and these he called his books. If you had read in Moses' book, you must have unrolled it as you read it.

When Moses had done writing his books, he called the priests, and told them to take care of them. Moses said to them: You must read these books to all the Israelites, to the men, the women, and the little children, that they may know how to please God.

Moses wished that some good man should take care of the

Israelites after he was dead; for he loved them very much, though they had behaved ill to him. So Moses begged God to give them to the care of some good man; and God heard his prayer, and said to Moses: I have found a man who will take care of the children of Israel after you are dead.

Who do you think this man was? It was Joshua, one of the good spies; he had helped Moses to do God's work for forty years, so that Moses had taught him a great deal. Moses was glad that Joshua would take up his work.

Moses called Joshua, and said to him: God will let you take the children of Israel into Canaan; you must be very brave, for you will have to fight against the wicked people; but God will help you, so do not be afraid. God will never leave you, nor forsake you.

Moses wished to speak to the people before he died, and advise them to be good; so Moses called all the people together, and told them he was going to die. I am very old, said he; I am a hundred and twenty years old this day. I offended God, and I must not go into the land of Canaan; but Joshua will take you there. Remember to obey God, and to love Him, and he will always bless you; but if you worship idols, and are wicked, God will punish you.

God told Moses to teach the people a song, that they might sing it after he was dead.

After Moses had taught the people the song, he blessed them, and left them forever.

God said to Moses: Go up that high mountain alone. I cannot let you go into Canaan, but I will let you see the beautiful land of Canaan from the top of that mountain.

THE DEATH OF MOSES.

MOSES' VIEW OF THE PROMISED LAND.

Moses was glad that he might see Canaan, though he might not go in. So Moses went up the mountain alone. He was very old, yet he was not weak; he could walk as well as when he was young, and he could see as well, for his eyes were not dim; he read and wrote, and saw things far off.

I think the Israelites must have felt very sad when they saw Moses go up all alone, and when they knew they should see him no more.

When Moses was at the top of the hill, he looked and saw the land of Canaan a great way off. It was a beautiful land,

MOSES.

full of green hills and rivers, of fields ripe with corn, trees laden with fruit.

When Moses had looked at the land, he died. No friend was near to close his eyes, or to hear his last sigh.

God himself buried Moses, not upon the top of the hill, but in some secret place under the hill. No one knows where Moses lies but the angels, who carried his soul to God.

PLOWING IN EGYPT.

CHAPTER XXXVI.

JOSHUA, OR RAHAB.

The Israelites were now close to the land of Canaan. They were sorry that Moses was dead; but Joshua was left to take care of them, and tell them what to do. God would speak to Joshua, and he would tell them what God said.

The Israelites would soon have to fight the wicked people who lived in Canaan. God chose that they should be killed for their wickedness, and God chose that the Israelites should live in their land instead of them.

There was a great river between the wilderness and Canaan which the Israelites would be obliged to cross. They could see the green hills of Canaan on the other side of the river, and they saw a great town also, with high walls all round it. This town was called Jericho. It was in Canaan, and wicked people lived in it. The Israelites knew that they would soon have to fight against the people who lived in this town.

Joshua told two of the Israelites to go to the town, and to come back, and tell him about it, and about the people. These men were called spies, because they were sent to spy, or look at the town.

Joshua did not wish the people of Jericho to know when these two spies came into the town, lest the wicked people should kill them. So they went when it was almost dark. The spies got over the river; there was one place in the river where the water was not very deep, and where people could get over. This was called a ford.

The gate of Jericho used to be shut when it was dark; but the spies came just before the gate was shut. They went to the house of a woman named Rahab, who kept an inn. Her house was built upon the wall of Jericho. Some people had seen them, and these people went and told the king of Jericho that two Israelites were in Rahab's house. The king of Jericho knew that the Israelites meant to come and fight against him; so he wanted to kill these two spies, and he sent some men to Rahab's house to get them. But God put it into Rahab's heart to be kind to them. Rahab had taken the spies to the top of her house to hide them. The

ON THE HOUSE TOP.

roof of her house was not slanting, like the roof of your house; it was flat, like the floor. On the roof of Rahab's house there were a great many stalks of flax. Flax is a plant; and its stalks are made into thread. Rahab had spread these stalks upon the roof of her house to dry. When the spies had climbed up the stairs, she told them to lie down; and she covered them over with the stalks, so that no one could see them.

The men who went to bring the spies to the king of Jericho, could not find them; so they looked for them outside the city, among the hills, and by the riverside.

When the king of Jericho's men were gone, Rahab crept up the stairs to speak to the spies. It was night, so she could talk to them on the roof without being seen. The men came from

…der the heaps of flax. Rahab had been taught to worship idols; but you see that she now believed in the true God, and not in idols. She was very much afraid lest, when the Israelites should come over the river to fight against Jericho, they would

ESCAPE OF THE TWO SPIES.

kill her and her friends; so she begged the spies to save her and those she loved.

Poor Rahab said: I know that God will let the people of Israel come and live in Canaan. Everybody is frightened lest you should kill them. We have heard how your God helped you to pass through the Red Sea. I know that your God is

JOSHUA, OR RAHAB.

the only true God. I have been kind to you, and will you be kind to me?

The spies said: If you will not tell anybody about our having come here, we promise to save your life, and the life of your father and mother, and brothers and sisters.

Then Rahab helped the spies to get out of the town. It was night, and the gates were shut. If the spies waited till morning, the people of Jericho would see them going out, and would kill them; but Rahab found a way of letting them go.

RAHAB'S WINDOW.

Her house was built on the wall of Jericho; one of the windows in her house looked toward the green hills outside of Jericho. This window was high; so Rahab took a rope, and tied the rope round one of the men, and let him down from the window; and then she tied the rope round the other man, and let him down.

When the men were standing on the ground outside the wall of Jericho, they called to Rahab, who was looking out of the window, and said: Take that red rope, and bind it to your window; bring your father and mother, and brothers and sisters, into your house.

CHAPTER XXXVII.

JOSHUA, OR THE RIVER JORDAN.

The people of Israel were now close to Canaan; but a deep river ran between the wilderness and Canaan—the river Jordan. How were the Israelites to get over the river?

You shall hear what God told Joshua to do.

Joshua rose up early in the morning, and he said to the people: Look and see where the priests take the ark, and follow them; but do not go too near.

Then Joshua said to the priests: Take up the ark, and walk on.

The ark was a golden box, covered with a blue cloth, that none might see it, or see the golden angels on the top. Two long sticks were run through little rings joined in the ark, and the priests held the ends of the sticks.

The priests took up the ark when Joshua bade them. They went to the edge of the water, not knowing what they were to do. They were dressed in white, and their feet were bare.

Joshua called to them to stand still. Then he said to the people: You will see a great wonder that God is going to do; when the priests put their feet in the water, a dry path shall be made.

All the people had come out of their tents.

They had got all their things ready for the journey, and were looking at the priests.

As soon as the priests touched the water, it stood up like a wall on each side, and there was a dry path made through the river. The priests walked along, till they came to the middle of the river; then they stopped, and Joshua said to the people: Now, pass over Jordan.

While the people were crossing, the priests stood still in the middle of the river. At last, all the people got over into the

ISRAEL CROSSING THE RIVER JORDAN DRY SHOD.

land of Canaan, except twelve men that Joshua had told to stay on the other side.

Joshua said to them: See where the priests are standing; there are great stones lying near them; take up twelve great stones, and bring them over with you into Canaan. These

ISRAELITES PASSING JORDAN.

twelve men walked through the dry path; each took up a great stone in his arms, and carried it to the other side. Then Joshua said to them: Put the twelve stones by the side of the river in Canaan.

The stones were to be put there that the people might never forget this great wonder of making a path in Jordan.

ISRAELITES BEING CARRIED.

God knew, that a long time afterward, little children would see the twelve stones, and would say to their fathers: What are these stones for?

Then their fathers would say: These stones were once at the bottom of the water; but God made a path for us, and we

JOASH READING THE LAW.

have put the stones here, to keep God's kindness in our minds.

All the time the twelve men were walking through with the stones, the priests were standing still in the river.

At last Joshua said to the priests: Come up out of Jordan. So the priests came up out of the river. When they put their feet on the dry land, the water rolled back again, and the river looked as it had done before.

How happy the Israelites must have been. They had wandered forty years in the wilderness, but at last they had arrived safely in Canaan. God had been very good to them, and he would help them to fight against the wicked people of Canaan.

The king of Jericho saw the Israelites come over the river. He could look at them from his high walls. He was very much frightened, and so were all the people in Jericho. Only Rahab was not frightened; she knew she was safe; she believed in the true God.

The priests put down the ark; all the Israelites set up their tents, and waited outside Jericho.

The gates of Jericho were kept fast shut, that the Israelites might not get in; no one in Jericho went out, and no one came in.

CHAPTER XXXVIII.

JOSHUA, OR THE WALLS OF JERICHO.

The children of Israel had placed their tents all round the city of Jericho, but they waited till God told them what to do. They could not get through the strong gates, unless God helped them.

Joshua was the captain of the Israelites. He was very brave. He trusted in God to help him.

One day Joshua, when outside of Jericho, looked up and saw a man standing before him a little way off. The man looked like a soldier, and he held a sword in his hand. Joshua knew that this man was not one of the Israelites; but he could not tell who he was.

Joshua went up to the man, and said: Are you come to help us fight; or are you come to help the people of Jericho?

The man answered: I am come as captain of the army of the Lord.

Now Joshua knew who this man was.

He was greater than a man, greater than an angel. He was the Lord from heaven, even Jesus Christ.

When Joshua knew who the man was, he fell down with his face upon the ground, and worshiped Him, saying: What will my Lord say to His servant?

Joshua called himself God's servant.

Then the great Captain of God's army said to Joshua in a loud voice: Take your shoes from off your feet, because this is holy ground where you stand.

Then Joshua took them off, and waited to know what the Lord would say to him.

Why was the ground holy? Because God was there. You know the priests wore no shoes when they walked in God's house.

The Lord told Joshua how he was to fight against Jericho.

A LEVITE.

Such a way of fighting was never known before.

When the Lord had gone back to heaven, Joshua called the priests, and all the people of Israel, and showed them what they must do. Joshua told some of the priests to take up the ark,

184   JOSHUA, OR THE WALLS OF JERICHO.

Then he called seven more priests, and said: Each of you must take a ram's horn, and blow with it, like a trumpet, and walk before the ark. You know that a ram is a sheep, and has crooked horns.

Then Joshua called all the soldiers, and told them to go

DESTRUCTION OF JERICHO.

before the priests, and he told the rest of the people that had no swords or spears, that is, the women and children, to walk behind the priests.

You never saw such a great number of people walking along.

Before they set out, Joshua told them not to make any shoutings, but to wait till he said, Shout.

Soldiers shout when they have conquered. The Israelites were not to shout till Joshua told them.

The people of Jericho heard the trumpets blowing, and they saw the men with swords and spears.

I dare say they thought the Israelites were going to shoot their arrows over the walls, and try and beat down the walls. Rahab took care to keep in her house, with all her dear friends. The Israelites walked once round Jericho, and then Joshua brought them back to their tents.

The next day Joshua made the people and the priests walk round once more, and then brought them home again. Then, next day after, they went round again; and the next day, and the next day. Six days, one after the other, they walked round Jericho, and came home to their tents again, without having fought.

The Israelites behaved well in doing as Joshua told them, instead of asking why they must walk round.

At last, after six days, Joshua told the Israelites to get up very early, as soon as it was light. He told them to walk all round as before; but when they had walked round, he did not tell them to go back to their tents, but to walk round again. That day they walked round seven times; they spent the whole day in walking round and round the city of Jericho.

When they had finished walking round the seventh time, Joshua said to the people: Now when the priests blow again with the trumpets, you may shout; for God has given you the city. You will soon get in; you must kill all the people except

Rahab and her friends that are in her house. You will find many beautiful things in Jericho; but you must not keep anything yourselves; but you must bring the cups of gold and silver and brass and iron to the Lord; bring all you find to the house of the Lord.

When Joshua had done speaking, the priests blew again with the trumpets, and the people gave a great shout. At the same moment, the walls of Jericho fell down. How horrible was the crash of those great walls. Now the men of Jericho saw that the day had come when they must die.

The two spies ran quickly to Rahab's house, and brought her out, and her father and mother, and brothers and sisters; and led them to a safe place near the tents of the Israelites. Rahab and her friends brought all their things with them out of the house, so they could make tents and live together.

But what happened to the people in Jericho? They were all killed; the men, the women and the children. The Israelites killed them with their swords. Then they set fire to the houses, and burnt them up; but the cups and basins made of gold and silver and brass and iron, they brought to the priests for God's house.

All the other people in Canaan heard about Jericho, and they were more frightened than before. They said: What a great captain Joshua is!

CHAPTER XXXIX.

JOSHUA—HIS DEATH.

There were a great many other cities in Canaan besides Jericho. The Israelites fought against the other cities.

All the people in Canaan heard of it, and were afraid of Joshua; but still they took their swords and spears, and fought against him.

God always helped the Israelites; so they always conquered. They went all through Canaan. First they went to one city, and slew the people in it, as God had commanded them to do; then they went to another city, and slew the people in it; so they went to many cities, till they

FRUITS OF PALESTINE.

JOSHUA—HIS DEATH.

had slain a large part of the people in Canaan. God did not make the walls of the other cities to fall down, like the walls of Jericho; but the Israelites were obliged to fight very hard before they could get in.

At last Joshua said to the children of Israel: Now the people of Canaan are dead, I will give you places to live. So he gave to each of the Israelites a house, full of nice and convenient things; a garden, a field, and a well of water.

Now the Israelites rested. They sat down under the fig-trees and vines in their own gardens, and ate the figs and grapes that grew on them, and they drank water out of the wells in their gardens.

The Israelites lived in the houses of the people of Canaan. The wicked people had built the houses, and dug the wells, and planted the trees in the garden; but God had taken them away from these wicked people, and had given them to the Israelites.

FIG TREE AND FRUIT.

There was one thing which Joshua did not forget to do, that was to place the tabernacle in Canaan. He set it up at a place called Shiloh. The Israelites would not be obliged to move it about any more.

Joshua told them to come up and worship God in the

JOSHUA—HIS DEATH.

tabernacle; but some lived so far off that they could not come often. So they came occasionally to the tabernacle.

God warned the Israelites not to worship the idols that the wicked people had made. The Israelites would find these idols in the fields and gardens, and some were made of silver and gold; but they were not to keep them, even if they were pretty; they were not to take the idols into their houses, but were to burn them in the fire, because God hated idols.

At last Joshua grew very old, and he knew that he must die. So he called a great many of the Israelites together, that he might speak to them.

He stood near a great oak tree while he spoke. He said: I am soon to die. After I am dead, will you worship idols, or will you worship God, who has been so kind to you?

They all said: We will worship God.

Then Joshua said: If you choose to worship God, you must not worship idols too.

Then they answered: We will serve God.

Now, said Joshua, you have promised to serve God only. You must keep your promise.

Then Joshua took a book and wrote down what the people had said. Afterward Joshua took a great stone, and set it up under the oak, and said: See this stone; I have put it here to make you remember your promise.

Very soon afterward Joshua died. He was more than a hundred years old.

CHAPTER XL.

SAMUEL, OR THE PIOUS MOTHER.

You have heard how the Israelites came into Canaan. I shall now tell you what happened to them in Canaan, after Joshua was dead.

HANNAH'S PRAYER.

You remember that the tabernacle was placed in Shiloh. The high-priest lived in Shiloh, that he might offer sacrifices in the tabernacle.

LITTLE SAMUEL LEFT IN THE TEMPLE.

I am now going to tell you of a high-priest called Eli.

Eli was a very good old man. A great many people used to come up every year to Shiloh, to worship God in the tabernacle.

Among the people who came up to worship, was a man who had two wives. People might have two wives a long while ago, though they must not have two now.

One of these wives was a very good woman; her name was Hannah, but she had no child. The other wife was unkind and wicked; but she had many children. The unkind wife laughed at Hannah, and said that God gave Hannah no child because He did not love her. This was not true, for God loved Hannah very much. Poor Hannah used sometimes to cry when the other wife spoke unkindly to her.

Once, when Hannah came to Shiloh, and the other wife had been laughing at her, she went to the tabernacle to pray to God. Eli was in the court of the tabernacle. He was sitting upon a high seat, and saw her come into the court. Now Hannah was praying to God in a very low voice, and her eyes were red with weeping. When Eli saw her, he thought she had been drinking wine, and spoke roughly. But she answered very meekly, and said: I have not been drinking wine; I have been praying to God, for I am very unhappy.

When Eli heard this, he spoke kindly, and said: May God give you what you have been asking for.

She had been praying for a little child, and she had been promising God to bring him up to serve God, and to teach people about God.

Hannah was very glad when Eli spoke so kindly to her, and

SAMUEL AND HIS COAT.

she wiped away her tears, and she went home looking quite happy; and God gave her a little babe, and she called his name Samuel.

While Samuel was a babe, Hannah did not go up to Shiloh; but when he was a little child about three or four years old, she took him up to Shiloh with her.

Hannah did not forget her promise to teach her child about God; and she did not mean to keep him always at home with her, though she loved him very much. She wished the good old high-priest Eli to bring him up, and teach him. So she brought the child to Eli, and said: I am the woman that you once saw in the court of the tabernacle, praying to God; I was praying for this child, and God has heard my prayer, and I wish the child to be brought up to serve God.

Eli took the little boy to live with him. Hannah sung a beautiful song of praise to God for His goodness in hearing her prayers, and then she left her dear little Samuel, and she went home again with her husband.

Do you think she ever came to see her child? Yes, every year, and she always brought him a present of a dress, such as the people wore in those days. It was a linen dress, and had long sleeves. God had put His spirit into Samuel's heart. He liked serving the Lord in the tabernacle, and seeing the sacrifices offered, and hearing the Lord praised. As he grew older, he pleased God more and more, and a great many people loved him. How glad Hannah must have been when she came to see him, to hear that he was a good child. It makes your parents, dear children, very happy to hear that you are good.

CHAPTER XLI.

SAMUEL, OR THE LITTLE PROPHET.

Eli and Samuel did not live in the tabernacle, but in some tents very near it. Eli had two sons, who were grown-up men, and they were priests, and offered sacrifices at the altar.

I suppose you think that Eli's sons were good, because Eli was good; but I am sorry to tell you that they were wicked men. They did not love God; they only cared for eating, and amusing themselves.

Eli heard of the wicked things that his sons did; and he said: Why do you do such wicked things? Everybody tells me of your wickedness. Oh! my sons, the Lord will be very angry, and will punish you. But they would not mind what their father said, but went on in their bad ways.

At last a good man came to Eli, and told him that God was very angry, and that he would let both his sons be killed in one day.

One evening old Eli was lying in bed; and little Samuel was lying in another bed a little way off. Samuel heard a voice calling him: Samuel! Samuel thought that Eli called him, and he answered: Here am I. And then he got out of bed and ran to Eli, to know what he wanted. See what a kind little child Samuel was, and how ready he was to wait upon old Eli.

But Eli said to Samuel: I did not call you. Then Samuel went and lay down again.

Soon afterward Samuel heard some one calling again; so he

went again and said: Here am I. But Eli said: I did not call, my son; lie down again.

Then Samuel lay down, and he soon heard the voice again, saying: Samuel! Then he felt sure that it was Eli who called him, and he went to him and said: Here am I.

Eli told Samuel to lie down again, and when he heard the voice, to answer: Speak, Lord, for Thy servant heareth. Samuel was to call himself God's servant.

So Samuel went and lay down again, and soon the Lord came and stood by him, and called as before: Samuel, Samuel! Then Samuel answered: Speak, for Thy servant heareth. God had never spoken to Samuel before. Samuel must have longed to know what He had to say to him. It was something sad and dreadful; it was about Eli.

God told Samuel that He should soon punish Eli's sons for their wickedness, and that he was displeased with Eli for not having punished them.

After God had done speaking, Samuel remained in his bed, and Eli did not call him.

So when the morning came, Samuel began to open the doors round about the tabernacle; for it was his business to open the doors. Soon Eli called Samuel; he wanted to know what God had said to him. Eli begged Samuel to tell everything to him, and to hide nothing from him. Then little Samuel told Eli all that God had said.

After this, God often spoke to Samuel, and told him how He would punish wicked people; and Samuel used to tell people what God had said. All that Samuel told them came true. He was a prophet. A prophet is a person to whom the

Lord tells what He means to make happen, so that he can tell others and warn them.

People paid great attention to what Samuel said, but still many people went on doing wicked things. The people in Shiloh were very wicked, and God determined soon to punish them, as well as Eli's sons.

LILY OF PALESTINE

CHAPTER XLII.

SAMUEL, OR THE ARK IN THE BATTLE.

I shall tell you soon how God punished Eli's sons; but first I must speak to you of some people who lived in the land of Canaan, called the Philistines.

They were wicked people, who worshiped idols, and hated the Israelites; they often fought against the Israelites, and took away their things. When God was pleased with the Israelites, He did not let the Philistines hurt them.

One day a great number of Philistines came out of their towns to fight against the Israelites. They brought tents, and slept in them at night. The Israelites heard that the Philistines were coming to fight against them; so a great number of them took their swords and spears, and placed their tents near the tents of the Philistines. In the morning the Philistines and the Israelites fought with each other. God did not help the Israelites, as he used to do, so the Israelites were frightened, and ran back into their tents.

Now the Israelites ought to have prayed to God; but instead of praying, they said. Let us send for the ark of God. If the ark were here, we should be able to conquer the Philistines.

You remember that the ark was a golden box, on which God sometimes sat in a cloud.

The Israelites sent a man to Shiloh to ask the priests to bring the ark. The sons of Eli were priests. They brought the ark to the tents of the Israelites. When the Israelites saw the ark, they were delighted, and they gave a very loud shout to show their joy. The shout could be heard a great way off. The Philistines heard the shout, and they asked why the Israelites shouted. Soon they heard that the ark of the God of Israel was come to the tents of the Israelites. Then the Philistines were afraid, and said, If the God of the Israelites

DEATH OF ELI.

should help them, what should we do? for their God once killed Pharaoh and all his men, and He could kill us too. Oh! let us be very brave, and let us fight with all our strength.

So the Philistines and the Israelites came out of their tents to fight, and the priests brought the ark on their shoulders.

But God did not help the Israelites. A great many of them were killed; and the two sons of Eli were killed, as God had said.

The Philistines took the ark of God. How pleased they were to get it! They carried it back to the towns where they lived.

Eli had not come to the battle. He had staid in Shiloh; he was very unhappy about the ark. He wanted to know what had become of it; so he sat upon a high seat just at the gate of Shiloh.

At last a man came running along the road; he had been fighting in the battle, and he came to tell the people in Shiloh all that had happened. He had put dust upon his head, and had torn his clothes, to show that he had sad news to tell. But Eli was old and blind, and did not see the man. When the man told the people in Shiloh what had happened, the people cried out very loud with grief; and Eli heard them crying, and asked why they cried; then the man answered, I am just come from where the Israelites were fighting. A great many Israelites have been killed, and your two sons are dead, and the ark of God is taken.

When Eli heard this he was very unhappy; he was sitting on a high seat that had no back, and he fell backward in his grief and broke his neck; for he was a very old man, and very heavy. He was almost a hundred years old.

How grieved Samuel must have been when he heard how Eli had died!

CHAPTER XLIII.

SAMUEL, OR THE GOD DAGON.

The Philistines were much delighted at getting the ark, for they knew it belonged to a great God. The Philistines took the ark to one of their cities, and put it in the house of their idol. This idol's name was Dagon. The Philistines had made an image like a man, and they called it Dagon; they had built a house for Dagon, and had set Dagon up on a high place. They used to come and worship very often in this house.

The Philistines left the ark all night in the house of Dagon: the next morning they got up early, and went into the idol's house. But what do you think they saw when they went in? They saw their idol Dagon fallen down from the high place, and lying upon his face prostrate before the ark.

God had thrown Dagon down. He wished to show the Philistines that He was stronger than idols.

The Philistines were not sure that it was God who had done this; so they lifted up Dagon and set him in his place again, and left him.

The next morning they rose early, and came into the idol's house.

Again Dagon had fallen down upon his face before the ark; and this time Dagon was broken; his head and his hands were broken off. The Philistines were sorry their idol was broken. I do not know whether they mended their idol, or whether they set him up again; but God soon made something much worse happen to the Philistines. God made them very ill indeed, and full of pain. They said to one another, What shall we do with the ark? for it shall not stay in this city any longer. So they sent it to another city, where some other Philistines lived.

But they fell very ill indeed, and a great many died. So the people of that city sent it to another city. The people of the other city were frightened when they saw the ark coming. They said, We too shall die, now the ark is brought here.

Soon they fell very ill, and a great many of them died, and the city was full of people groaning and crying.

At last the Philistines thought they would send the ark back to the Israelites; but they did not feel quite sure that the God of Israel had been angry with them for keeping the ark.

They made a plan for sending it back. Their plan was this: We will take two cows that have never drawn a cart before; and we will tie them to the cart, and we will shut up their calves. No one shall drive the cows, but we will see what they will do. If the cows leave their calves, and go to the place where the Israelites live, then we shall be quite sure that it was the God of Israel who made us so ill, to punish us for keeping the ark.

This was the plan of the Philistines. They had heard how God once sent plagues on Pharaoh. They said, We will not harden our hearts, as Pharaoh and the people of Egypt did.

The Philistines took two cows and tied them to the cart, then laid the ark upon the cart, and watched to see what the cows would do.

Then God made the cows do a wonderful thing. They drew the cart, without being driven, along the road which led to the place where the Israelites lived. They lowed as they went, and never once turned out of the road.

Some of the Philistines followed the cart.

At last the cart came to a place where some of the Israelites were reaping corn in a field. They looked up, and saw the cart coming, and they saw the ark, and then they were glad indeed. The cows brought the cart into the field, and then stopped by the side of a great stone.

The Philistines were much surprised at the wonderful thing that God had done, and they went back to their own land. Don't you think, dear children, they should have left off worshiping idols, when they saw how great the God of Israel was?

They should have burned their idols, and only worshiped the true God. But they went on worshiping idols, and God was angry with them for it.

The Israelites did a thing that displeased God. They looked into the ark. God did not allow any one to do this. The book of stone in which the ten commandments were written was inside the ark.

God is angry when people dare to disobey Him; He made those Israelites fall ill, and they were afraid of keeping the ark in their city; so they sent messages to some other Israelites to take it. They did so, and put it in the house of a man who lived upon a hill. He and his son took care of it.

The ark was not sent back to the tabernacle at Shiloh because God was angry with the people at Shiloh for all their wickedness. The people in Shiloh had worshiped idols, and so God would not let the ark go back to Shiloh.

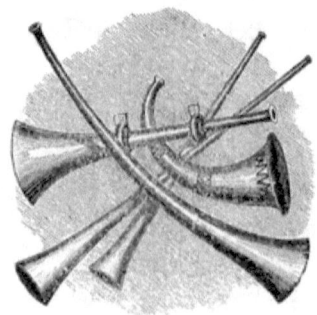

ANCIENT TRUMPETS.

CHAPTER XLIV.

SAUL, OR THE KING.

When Samuel was grown up he was called a judge ; but he was not king. He used to tell the people what God wished them to do ; and he used to punish bad people. Moses had once been the judge of Israel, and Joshua had once been the judge, and Eli had once been the judge. Now, Samuel was the judge. He did not sit on a throne or wear a crown, as kings do. He always asked God to tell him what the people ought to do. The Israelites ought to have been very glad that God was their king. No other king was as good and as great as He.

You will be sorry to hear that at last they grew tired of having God for their King. They said, We should like to have a king that would go out to battle before us. They wanted to have a king that they could see. So they came to Samuel, and said, Give us a king.

Samuel was very sorry to hear this, and he went and prayed to the Lord. God was displeased with them for wishing for a king; but as they wanted a king He said they should have one.

So Samuel called the Israelites together, and said, God will let you have a king ; but he will not treat you as well as God has. He will make your sons to work for him; some will run before his chariots; some will make swords for him; some will plow his ground, and reap his corn. He will take away many of your fields and gardens, and give them to whom he pleases; and then you will be sorry that you wished for a king, and you will cry to God, and He will not hear you.

Still the Israelites wished for a king. They would not mind what Samuel said; but they cried out, We will have a king.

God was to choose the king.

There was a young man whose father had some fields, and sheep, and cows, and horses. One day three horses were lost; so the young man went to look for them among the hills. The young man's name was Saul. He took a servant with him, and looked for the horses a long while, but he could not find them. At last Saul came near the city where Samuel lived.

The servant said to Saul, I have heard that there is a man in that city who is a prophet: all he says comes true. Let us ask him where the horses are. Then Saul said to his servant, Come, let us go. So they went into the city, and as they went along they met Samuel. They had never met Samuel before; so they did not know who he was. Samuel was an old man, and his hair was long, and he used to wear a cloak.

Saul spoke to this old man, and said, Can you tell me where the prophet's house is?

Samuel answered, I am the prophet.

Samuel knew who Saul was. Though Samuel had never seen him before, God had told Samuel that he would meet a man just at that time who would be the king of Israel.

Before Saul had told him what he wanted, Samuel said, The horses that you lost three days ago are found. And Samuel told Saul that he had a great deal to say to him, and that he must come home with him that evening.

So Saul and the servant went to Samuel's house, and Samuel took Saul to the top of his house, and talked to him alone.

The next morning they all got up very early, and Samuel

walked with Saul and the servant through the city. When they were come to the outside of the city, Samuel said to Saul, Bid the servant pass on before. So the servant passed on, and Samuel and Saul stood still together.

Then Samuel took a bottle of oil, that he had brought with him, and poured it on Saul's head, and said, God has chosen thee to be king over Israel.

Samuel poured the oil upon Saul's head as a sign that he was to be the king. Pouring oil upon a person is called anointing him.

After Samuel had anointed Saul they parted. Saul went on his way, and returned to his friends: but he did not tell any one that he was to be the king of Israel.

Soon afterward Saul called all the Israelites together, and showed the people who was to be their king. When the people saw Saul they were very much pleased, for he was taller than any of the Israelites; no one else reached higher than his shoulder. The Israelites wished to have a king that would look very grand when he went out to battle.

The Israelites shouted when they saw him, and cried out, God save the king!

CHAPTER XLV.

SAUL, OR THE DISOBEDIENT DEED.

I have told you how God made Saul the king of Israel. Saul sat upon a throne, wore a crown, and went to battle in a chariot. He was brave, and could fight well against wicked soldiers who tried to hurt the Israelites.

Samuel used to come and see him, and advise him to serve God. Samuel wished Saul to be good, and he often prayed for him.

At last God chose to see whether Saul would do all He desired him to do. You remember how God once tried Abraham; and how Abraham did what God desired him, because he loved God.

There were some wicked people who lived near the land of Canaan, called the Am-a-lekites. God was displeased with them.

One day Samuel came to Saul, and said, God commands you to go and fight against the Amalekites, and kill them all.

Saul got a great army of Israelites, and went to the Amalekites, and conquered them. Then Saul ordered his soldiers to kill them with their swords, as God had told him. But he thought he should like to take the king of the Amalekites back to Canaan with him; so he would not let him be killed. I think Saul liked to bring the king home with him, because he thought it was a grand and fine thing to have a king shut up near him in Canaan. Neither did Saul kill the fat and strong oxen and sheep; he only killed those that were thin and weak. Saul wished to be rich, and to have a great many cattle.

That night God spoke to Samuel, and told him that He was much displeased with Saul.

Samuel was grieved, and prayed all night.

The next morning Samuel went to Saul, for God had told him many things to say.

Saul did not know that Samuel knew of his wickedness, and tried to make him think that he had done as God had told him.

When Saul saw Samuel he pretended to be glad to see him, and said, I have done the commandment of the Lord. Then Samuel said, What is this bleating of sheep and lowing of oxen that I hear?

Now Saul saw that it would be of no use to say that he had not saved the sheep and oxen, so he began to make excuses for himself.

Then Samuel told Saul that God was angry with him, and did not intend that he should be king much longer.

Saul was much frightened when he heard that God would punish him, and said, Stay and pray to God with me. But Saul was not really sorry; he was only afraid of being punished. Samuel knew this, and would not stay. Then Saul took hold of Samuel's cloak, to hinder him from going away, and tore the cloak.

Samuel stopped, and said to Saul, God has torn the land of Canaan from you, and He has given it to a man that is better than you are. God has done it already, and He will not change His mind.

Saul begged Samuel very much to stay and to pray with

SAUL, OR THE DISOBEDIENT DEED.

SAUL TEARING THE ROBE OF SAMUEL.

him, that the people might not know that God was angry. You see that Saul cared more about what people thought than about God's being pleased with him.

Finally Samuel consented to stay a little while, and then left him.

CHAPTER XLVI.

DAVID, OR THE YOUNG SHEPHERD.

Samuel did not know whom God intended to make king instead of Saul. God said to him, Fill a horn with oil, and go to Jesse who lives in Bethlehem, for I have chosen one of his sons as the king.

Jesse was an old man, and had many sons, who were grown men. Samuel found Jesse and his sons in Bethlehem.

Now the eldest son was a tall, fine-looking man, who seemed fit to be a king, and Samuel thought to himself, Surely this is the one that God will choose.

But God told Samuel that He had not chosen him. God does not care how a person looks, but he cares for the heart. Now the heart of Jesse's oldest son did not please God, and this time God was going to choose a king who loved Him in his heart.

Then Samuel looked at Jesse's second son ; but God had not chosen him. Then Samuel looked at the third son ; but God had not chosen him. Then at the fourth, neither had God chosen him; then at the fifth, next at the sixth, and last of all, at the seventh; and yet God had not chosen any of them.

So Samuel said to Jesse, Have you any more children ?

Jesse answered, I have one more child, the youngest, who is keeping the sheep. Then Samuel said, Send for him.

So Jesse sent for this youngest son.

The name of this son was David. He was only a boy. He

had a beautiful color on his cheeks, and his eyes had a pleasant look.

When he came in, God said to Samuel, Arise and anoint him, for this is he. So Samuel took the horn of oil and anointed him.

Then Samuel went to his own house.

You will hear a great deal about David. God did not mean that he should become king for a long while ; but David knew that he certainly should be king some day. He went on keeping his father's sheep. As he watched them he played on his harp, and sung sweet songs of praise to God. His songs are called psalms.

DAVID TENDING HIS SHEEP.

CHAPTER XLVII.

DAVID, OR THE HARP.

Samuel did not tell Saul who was to be king.

Yet Saul was unhappy. He felt uneasy, and could not rest. He lived in a fine house called a palace, but this did not make him happy; he had many servants, but they could do him no good.

Saul's servants saw that he had a wicked spirit, and they said, Shall we look for a man who can play very sweetly on the harp? Perhaps if you were to listen to sweet music, you might get well.

Then Saul told them to look for such a man.

One of the servants had heard of David, and he said, I have seen one of the sons of Jesse, who lives at Bethlehem; he can play beautifully on the harp; is a very brave young man, can speak wisely, and is handsome. God too, loves him: shall I send for him?

Saul said that he would like this young man. Some of Saul's servants went to Jesse and said, King Saul wishes to see your son David, who takes care of the sheep.

Jesse said that David might go; and he told David to take a present to King Saul. When Saul saw David he loved him very much. Perhaps Saul loved him because he had a sweet look, and could play well on the harp; but God loved him because he wished to please Him.

Saul liked David so much that he wished him to stay a long while, and to be near him.

David very often played to Saul upon the harp, and when David played he grew better, until at last he was quite well.

After a while David went away from Saul, and fed his father's sheep as he used to do.

I think David liked taking care of sheep better than living with Saul; for Saul was wicked, and many of his servants were wicked also.

David was happy when alone, thinking about God. Did you ever hear any of David's psalms? In one of his psalms he calls God his Shepherd. David took great care of his sheep, and led them to places where green fresh grass grew, and to smooth and clear water; and he made them lie down on the softest grass in cool places by the river's side. While David was taking so much care of his sheep he thought that God took still more care of him; and he said, The Lord is my Shepherd, I shall not want; He maketh me to lie down in green pastures, and beside still waters.

CHAPTER XLVIII.

DAVID, OR THE GIANT GOLIATH.

You remember who the Philistines were. They were wicked people, who lived in some of the cities of Canaan.

One day a great number of Philistines came, and placed their tents on the top of a hill in Canaan. When Saul heard it, he came with a great number of Israelites, and placed their tents on another hill. The Philistines and the Israelites could see each other, and they intended to fight, but they did not choose to fight at once.

There was one man among the Philistines whose name was Goliath. He was called a giant because he was ten feet high. He was very tall indeed.

He was very strong and big, and could fight well. He wore clothes made of iron and brass; people used to wear armor, that arrows and swords and spears might not hurt them easily.

He wore a cap of brass upon his head, and he wore a coat of iron: his legs were covered with brass. He held a great spear in his hand, and had a great sword by his side; and a man went before him with a shield. A shield is a great piece of iron or brass, like a large tray, which men used to hold before their faces in battle to prevent the arrows hurting them.

The giant thought that no one could kill him. Every day he used to call out with a loud voice, Will one of the Israelites come out and fight with me? If he is able to kill me, then all the Philistines will obey the king of Israel; but if I kill him, then the Israelites must obey the Philistines. Is there any man that will fight with me?

Would any of the Israelites fight with the giant?

No, not one. When Saul heard the Philistine giant, he was frightened, and all the Israelites were frightened. They all thought they should be killed, if they fought with him.

One day Jesse said to his son David, Go to the tents of Israel, and see how your brethren are.

So David rose up very early, and left his sheep with another shepherd, and went a long way, till he came to the hill where the tents of the Israelites were. Then he ran to look for his brothers. As he was talking, he heard a man speaking in a very loud voice. saying, Who is able to fight with me? It was the giant Goliath. David had never heard the giant speak before, but the people who were near David told him about the giant, and they said, King Saul has promised to give any man who kills the giant a great many things as a reward.

David was surprised that people should be afraid of fighting with the giant, because he knew that God could help an Israelite to conquer him, and he knew that the gods of the Philistines could not help them because they were idols; so David said, Who is this Philistine, that he should speak in this manner to the people of God? And David felt in his heart that he should not be afraid to fight with him.

Soon some one went and told Saul that there was a young man come who said he would fight with the giant. So Saul desired the young man to come before him. Saul had seen David before, but had forgotten him. Saul was surprised that David, who was so young, should wish to fight with the giant;

DAVID THROWING THE STONE.

and said, You are not able to fight with that Philistine; you are very young, and he has been used to fighting. Then David answered, Once when I was keeping my father's sheep, a lion came and took a lamb out of the flock, and I went after the lion and met him, and took the lamb out of his mouth; and when the lion tried to kill me, I caught him by his hair and killed him. And once a bear came, and I killed him too. I shall kill this Philistine, as I killed the lion and the bear. It was God who delivered me from the lion and the bear, and He will deliver me from this Philistine.

You see, David was not proud of his strength, but he knew that God could help him.

When Saul heard these words, he told him to go and fight the giant. But David had no sword, or coat of iron, so Saul lent him his own armor, and his own sword; he put a cap of brass on David's head, and dressed him in a coat of iron. But David had not been used to wear armor; so he said to Saul, I cannot wear this armor, and took it off again; neither would he take a sword, or a spear. He went to the brook and chose five smooth stones, and put them in a bag which he had, and took the bag with him. In the other hand he held a staff. Then David went to meet the giant.

The giant heard that one of the Israelites was ready to fight.

When the giant saw David he was surprised; he had expected to see a great man like himself, dressed in armor, and holding a spear in his hand.

But David was very young, and his face was rosy like a child's, and he only wore a shepherd's dress, and held a staff in his hand.

DAVID, OR THE GIANT GOLIATH.

The giant was angry when he saw him; then he began to laugh, and said, Come to me, and I will give your flesh to the birds.

But David was not afraid. He said, You have a sword, a spear, and a shield, but God will fight for me. He will help

DAVID AND GOLIATH.

me, and everybody will see that the God of Israel is the true God, and that He can save whom He pleases.

Then the giant came still nearer to David, and David ran toward him quickly, put his hand in his bag, drew out a stone, and put it in the sling that he had; then holding one end of the sling, he threw the stone with all his strength. It hit the giant in the forehead, and he fell upon the ground.

Then David ran to him, and taking the giant's sword, cut off his head. When the Philistines saw what a great wonder God had done, they were frightened; and the Israelites shouted, for they saw that their God fought for them.

David thanked God for helping him to conquer the giant. He sung God's praises, and played upon his harp. David did not wish people to praise him; he wished everybody to praise God. He wished all people to say, How great God is! He helped the poor young shepherd to conquer the great giant.

JONATHAN AND DAVID.

CHAPTER XLIX.

DAVID, OR THE JAVELIN.

Saul was glad that David had killed the giant. Saul said to David, Whose son are you, young man? And David answered, I am the son of Jesse, who lives at Bethlehem.

While Saul was talking to David there was a person standing near, of whom you have not heard; it was the son of Saul. He was very brave, and very good; his name was Jonathan; he was a prince, because he was the king's son, and the king's son is called a prince.

Jonathan began to love David very much indeed. He loved David because he was brave and good. David had also a very sweet look. Jonathan told David that he loved him, and they both promised to be kind to each other. Jonathan gave his own clothes to David, and wore other clothes; he also gave him his sword.

Saul told David that he must not go back to live with his father again, but must stay with him. So David and Jonathan saw each other often.

After the Philistines had been killed in battle, the Israelites went to their homes. Jonathan and David went with the king. As they were going along, they saw a great many women with harps, and they sung and danced. These are the words they sung: Saul has slain his thousands, and David his ten thousands.

David did not wish to be praised; he wished God to be praised. He would have liked to hear the women say that God had helped a poor shepherd to kill the giant.

But when Saul heard these songs he was angry; he wished to be praised, and could not bear to hear David praised more than himself. Do they say that David is braver than I am? How wicked Saul was. He was envious.

Saul thought, perhaps David is the man who is to be king

SAUL'S ATTEMPT TO KILL DAVID.

instead of me. He remembered that Samuel told him God had chosen a better man to be king.

Then Saul hated David, and wished to kill him. Saul had these wicked thoughts in his mind when he reached his own house. Instead of thanking God for his kindness in having helped the Israelites to conquer the Philistines, he was thinking how he could kill David.

David saw that Saul was ill, and unhappy.

He took his harp as he used to do, and began to play sweet music. Saul had a sharp thing in his hand called a javelin; and Saul thought, I will throw this at David, and it shall go through his body. But David saw the javelin coming, and slipped out of the way, so that Saul did not hurt him. Then Saul threw it again, but he could not hurt David. God took care of him.

Every one loved David, and this made Saul still more envious.

David behaved so well, that Saul could not find any fault for which to punish him. Then Saul told David to take some men, and to go and fight against the Philistines. Saul hoped that the Philistines would kill David in battle. David went, but no one hurt him. Everybody praised him more, and called him brave. Saul grew more angry. At last Saul told his servants to kill him, but they loved David, and would not. Jonathan was afraid lest some wicked person should mind Saul, and kill David; so Jonathan told David to hide, and said to his father, Why do you wish to kill David? What has he done? Did he not once kill the giant? Then you were glad: why are you angry with him now?

Saul promised that he would not have David killed. Then Jonathan called David and brought him to Saul, and David was with him as he used to be.

But soon Saul began to hate him again. Saul had a javelin in his hand, and threw it at David; but David slipped out of the way, and the javelin stuck in the wall.

Now David was afraid of staying any more with Saul; and he fled away that night.

He did not go back to his father; for Saul would have found him; but he hid in a great many places, and God took care of him.

DAVID SPARES THE LIFE OF SAUL.

CHAPTER L.

DAVID, OR THE CAVE.

When David fled from Saul he was obliged to leave his dear friend Jonathan. They kissed each other and shed many tears when they parted; but Jonathan chose to stay with his father, king Saul. There were very high hills in Canaan, and there were large holes in these hills, called caves, and in one of these David hid himself.

Very few people lived among these hills; but sheep fed on the fresh grass that grew on them, and goats leaped and sported on the tops of the hills.

David was not alone. His brothers came to him, besides a great many poor people. These people liked to be with David.

David and his friends lived together in a large cave, for some caves are very large, and will hold as many people as you see at church on Sunday.

Kind people gave them food. Saul was angry when he heard that all were kind to David. Saul used to tell people that David was wicked, and that David wished to kill him. Some people believed what Saul said, and thought David was really wicked.

Poor David! It made him sorry to think that people believed that he wanted to kill Saul. But it was a comfort to him that God knew he did not want to kill Saul. He sometimes asked God to look into his heart, to see whether he wished to kill Saul. David had his harp with him in the cave; he often sung psalms, and praised God for keeping him from being hurt.

DAVID, OR THE CAVE.

David did not always live in the same cave, lest wicked people should tell Saul where he was hid. Sometimes he hid among the thick trees in the wood, and sometimes in one cave, and sometimes in another.

Saul took a great many soldiers, and came to look for David among the hills, but God did not let Saul find him. Saul said to the people he met, Have you seen David and his men? If you love me, you will tell me where he is, for David wants to kill me. Then some people would tell Saul, He is in the cave in that hill. But when Saul got to the place he could not find David; for David had heard that Saul was looking for him, and had gone to another cave.

Saul was almost tired of looking for David, when something happened which you will like to hear.

Caves are dark inside, very dark; because, though there is a hole to go in at, there are no windows to let in the light. One day David was in a very large cave with his men, when Saul and his men passed that way. Saul did not know David was in the cave. But Saul saw the cave, and he wished to go in to sleep for a little while; so he left his men outside, and came in alone. David and his men saw him come in, but Saul did not see them, because they were in the dark parts of the cave. David and his men remained very quiet, and Saul lay down to rest. Then David's men said to him in a low

ENTRANCE TO CAVE.

voice, Now you can kill Saul if you wish it. No, said David, I will not hurt the man whom God made king. And David would not let his men hurt Saul; but he went gently up to Saul as he lay asleep, and cut off a piece of his clothes.

After a little while Saul rose up, and went out of the cave; and he and his men went on looking for David among the hills.

SEE THE SHIRT, ETC.

Then David came out of the cave, and called in a loud voice after Saul, My lord the king! Then Saul looked behind him, and David bowed himself down to the ground. Then David spoke very meekly to Saul, and said, Why do you think that I wish to kill you? You came into the cave where I was, and some people advised me to kill you; but I would not do it. Then David held up the piece of Saul's clothes that he had cut off. Look, my father, said David, at this; I cut it off. I could have killed you; but I would not. Why then do you hunt after me? The Lord will keep me safe, and will not let you hurt me.

When David had done speaking, Saul said, Is that your voice, my son David? And Saul began to weep. He had once loved David, and when he saw how good David was, he felt that he had been wicked; but he did not feel sorry that he had offended God.

Yes, said Saul, I see that you are much better than I am, and that you do not wish to kill me; and I know that you will be king one day.

So Saul did not try to kill David that day, and he left off looking for David, and went home with his men to his own house.

But David did not go and live with Saul, for he could not trust him. Once before, Saul had promised Jonathan that he would not try to kill David again, and yet he had broken his promise, and David knew that perhaps he would soon try to kill him again. So David went back to his cave.

CHAPTER LI.

DAVID, OR THE SPEAR.

Saul left off looking for David, but he soon began to hate him again. One day some wicked men came to him, and said, We can tell you where David has hid himself.

Saul was glad to hear where David was, and he took a great many soldiers with him and went to the place where he heard David was.

Saul directed his men to set up their tents on a hill, and to dig a deep ditch all round the tents, that nobody might come to the tents to hurt them. In the night Saul and his men would sleep in their tents, and in the daytime they would look for David.

Then David went with some of his friends near the place where the tents were, and he said to his friends, Who will go with me among the tents? And one of David's friends said, I will. Then David and his friend went in the night, and walked among the tents; but no one saw them or heard them; for God had made them sleep: even the people whom Saul had desired to watch, to prevent anybody coming, had fallen fast asleep. God did not choose that David should be hurt; therefore he made the people sleep.

David got over the great ditch that had been dug; for there was nobody watching near to hinder him.

David went into the tent of Saul. He found him sleeping; and by his pillow he saw his spear stuck into the ground, and a jug of water; and he saw other people who ought to have watched over him, asleep round about him.

Saul little knew that David was so near him, looking at him as he slept.

Then David's friend said to him, Let me take this spear and kill Saul; I will pierce his body through in a moment.

No, said David, do not kill him: it would be very wicked to kill the man whom God has made king. Only take the jug of water, and the spear, and let us go.

So they took the jug of water and the spear, and they went away from the tents; and nobody woke while they were passing.

You remember why David had once cut off some of Saul's clothes. It was for the same reason he now took the jug and spear. He wished to show Saul that he had been near his bed while he was asleep, and that he might have killed him, if he had chosen it.

Then David went down the hill where Saul's tents were, and went up another hill; so there was a great way between Saul and him. Then David cried out with a very loud voice to men that were sleeping round king Saul, and said, Why do you let people come near the king when he is asleep?

Then David showed the people the king's spear and the jug of water.

When Saul heard David's voice he remembered it, and wept.

He said, Is this thy voice, my son David?

And David said, It is my voice, O king. Why do you look for me? What have I done? Have any wicked men told you that I wish to hurt you?

Then Saul said, I have sinned. Go to your home again. I will never hurt you again, because you did not kill me to-day, when you might have done it. I have done very wickedly.

Then David said, Here is the king's spear. Send one of your servants to get it.

David would not bring the spear to Saul himself. He could not trust Saul; he was not sure that Saul would not kill him.

And then Saul went home, but David went into the part of Canaan where the Philistines lived, that Saul might not be able to hurt him.

David ought not to have gone to live with the Philistines, because they worshiped idols.

CHAPTER LII.

DAVID, OR THE PROMISE FULFILLED.

When Saul heard that David was gone to the Philistines, he went to look for him no more; because if Saul had gone to them, they would have tried to kill him.

The time had now almost come when Saul must die.

You know that the Philistines hated the people of Israel, and used to fight against them. One day the king of the Philistines called a great many of his soldiers together, and took them to a place in the land of Canaan where they might fight with the Israelites. When Saul heard they had come, he took his soldiers and went to fight against them. Saul's good son Jonathan went with his father to the battle.

The Philistines and the Israelites fought together upon some hills, and the Philistines conquered. God was angry with the Israelites, and he did not help them to conquer. The Israelites ran away from the Philistines; even Saul and Jonathan, though they were very brave, ran away; and the Philistines ran after them, and they killed Jonathan. Some men with bows and arrows shot at Saul, and some of the arrows went into his body, so that he could not run away any more; yet Saul was not killed by the arrows; he was only hurt.

When Saul found that he could not run away, he was afraid that the Philistines would get hold of him, and treat him very cruelly; so he wished very much to die before they overtook him. Then Saul said to one of his soldiers, Take your sword, and run it through my body.

234   DAVID, OR THE PROMISE FULFILLED.

The soldier would not kill Saul. Then Saul took his own sword, and fell upon the point of it; so it ran through his body, and he died.

The Philistines praised their idols, and said that their idols were greater than the God of Israel, because they said their

DEATH OF SAUL.

idols had helped them to conquer the Israelites. Then they took Saul's armor, and put it in one of the houses where they worshiped idols.

David all this time was in the land of the Philistines. He knew that Saul and Jonathan had been fighting a battle, and he

longed to know who had conquered. At last a man who h
been at the battle came to David, to tell him about it. The
man bowed down to David, and said, I come from the tents of
Israel.

Then David said, Pray tell me what has happened.

And the man said, The Israelites have run away, and many
are dead, and Saul and Jonathan are dead.

The man thought that David would have been very glad to
hear that Saul was dead. But David was not, for he still loved
Saul, and was sorry too that the Philistines had conquered him,
because he knew that the Philistines would praise their idols,
and speak against the God of Israel, and David loved God so
much, that he wished everybody to praise him. And David
was very sorry for Jonathan his friend. He would never see
his face again in this world.

David sung a sweet song about Saul and Jonathan. He said
that Saul and Jonathan had been like eagles and lions, they had
been so brave: he said they had lived together, and had died
together. And then he said in his song, I am distressed for
thee, my brother Jonathan; thy love to me was wonderful.
He called Jonathan his brother because he had been so very
kind to him.

David did not speak of Saul's wickedness, he only spoke
of his bravery; for he did not like to speak against the king.

Now the time had come when David was to be king. God
put it into the hearts of the Israelites to ask him to be their
king.

David praised God on his harp for keeping his promise, for
taking him from keeping sheep, and making him king over all

the iand   David wished to be a good king, and to do all that God told him, and to teach all his people to love God. He knew that God would bless him, and keep him from all harm.

SAMUEL ANOINTING DAVID

CHAPTER LIII.

DAVID, OR THE ARK ON ZION.

At last David was made king, as God had promised. David was born at Bethlehem, and there he kept sheep, but when he was king he lived at Jerusalem.

Jerusalem was a beautiful city. There were a great many hills in it. One of the hills was called Mount Zion.

David directed some men to build him a house upon Mount Zion. A king's house is called a palace.

David loved God very much, and so he thought he should like to have God's ark very near his palace.

You remember that the ark was once at Shiloh, and that the Philistines took it in battle, and that they sent it back to the Israelites: but the ark was never taken back to Shiloh. The ark had been kept in a man's house; David knew where it was, and he went himself to bring it. So they brought the ark from the man's house to Mount Zion in Jerusalem. David was dressed in a white ephod, and all the singers and players of music were dressed in white, and the priests were dressed in white.

David played upon his harp, and he went with the players and singers; and the ark came afterward with the priests.

A great many of the Israelites came to see this beautiful sight. They saw their king praising God upon his harp.

The ark was taken up the hill called Mount Zion. There were walls round the top of Mount Zion, and large gates; the gates were opened wide to let the king come in, and the ark, which was the throne of the Lord. David had made a new tabernacle, close to his own palace.

David also offered some sacrifices upon Mount Zion, and David blessed all the people that stood round.

Some used to sing in the day, and some used to sing in the night. The angels in heaven can sing night and day without resting, but these singers could not do so. When David was in his palace, he could hear them singing God's praise.

David wrote the psalms himself. He sung the psalms to his own harp, and he wrote them down, and sent them to the singers, that they might sing them near the ark.

David did not always stay in his palace on Mount Zion. He was often obliged to go out to fight against the Philistines, and God helped David and his men conquer them. Then David used to return to Mount Zion, and sing psalms to God for having helped him to conquer.

One day David was sitting in his beautiful palace, and he said to his friend Nathan, I live in a fine house, but God's ark is placed under curtains. And David wished to build a beautiful house for it.

Nathan, David's friend, was a very wise and a very good man, and he advised David to build a house for the Lord.

In the night God spoke to Nathan and said, Go tell David not to build me a house; I am pleased with David for wishing to build it, but I do not choose to have him build me one, because he has fought so many battles, and killed so many people; I will give David a son who shall build me a house.

Then Nathan came to David in the morning, and told him what God had said.

DAVID, OR THE ARK ON ZION.

David was much pleased to hear that God would bless him, and that he would give him a son who should build a house for God. So David went to thank God for his kind promises.

God liked David's prayer. David was not proud. He wondered that God should be kind to him, and that He should have taken him from being a shepherd to be a king.

Although David might not build a house for the Lord, it was his chief delight to make preparations so as to enable his sons to carry out his plans. He collected gold and silver in great quantities, and arranged with the king of Tyre to send him cedar from the mountains of Lebanon. The men of Tyre were famous sailors; they were the first to send ships around the Mediterranean Sea, and even beyond into the wide, unknown ocean.

SCENE AT TYRE.

CHAPTER LIV.

DAVID, OR URIAH'S WIFE.

David was a good man; he loved God, and tried to please Him. Yet there was still wickedness in David's heart, as well as goodness. I am going to tell you how David once displeased the Lord.

Once David's men went out to fight against some wicked people who lived near Canaan. David did not go himself to fight this time, but he told a man called Joab to take his soldiers to fight.

So David staid at Jerusalem. I do not know why he did not go out to fight himself.

One day when it was hot David lay upon his bed, and when it grew cool he got up and walked on the top of his house, which was flat and level like a floor. As he was walking there, he looked down and saw a woman whom he liked very much as soon as he saw her. David wished to have her for his wife; so he sent his servants to ask what her name was; and they came back and told him that her name was Bath-she-ba, and that she was married to a man called Uriah.

David ought to have prayed to God to keep him from thinking about Bathsheba any more; but he kept on thinking, and wishing that she could be his wife; and he thought, If Uriah was dead, then Bathsheba could be his wife. Now Uriah was a very brave and good man, and he had gone with Captain Joab a great way off to fight against some wicked people.

David wished that Uriah might get killed in the battle. At last a very wicked plan came into his heart. David wrote a letter to Joab the captain, and said, When you take the people out to fight, let Uriah stand in a place where the wicked people will shoot him.

David sent the letter to Joab. Joab ought not to have done

DAVID AND BATHSHEBA.

this wicked thing. But he was a very wicked man, so he determined to do as the king told him.

Soon afterward Joab took his soldiers to fight against a g eat city with walls all round it, and he told Uriah to go with some of the soldiers very near the walls of the city, and some of the men in the city shot arrows from the walls, and killed Uriah.

Then Joab sent a man to tell King David that Uriah was dead.

David was not sorry when he heard that Uriah was killed. He pretended to be sorry, but he felt glad in his heart. Now Bathsheba could be his wife; so he sent for Bathsheba, and married her, and she came and lived with him in his palace.

But God was displeased with what David had done.

One day Nathan, who was a prophet, came to David.

God had told Nathan what David had done.

Nathan began by telling David a little history. He said, There were two men in one city; the one was rich and the other poor; the rich man had a great many sheep; the poor man had only one little lamb, which he had taken care of since it was first born: he fed it and gave it drink out of his own cup, and he nursed it in his bosom, and loved it as one of his children. One day a visitor came to the rich man's house, and the rich man sent and took the poor man's lamb, and killed it, and prepared it for dinner for his visitor. Then said Nathan, What shall be done to the rich man?

And David felt very angry with the rich man, and he said to Nathan, He shall die; and he shall give the poor man four lambs instead of the one which he took.

Then Nathan said to David, Thou art the man.

Nathan did not mean that David was the man who had taken the poor man's lamb. David had not taken a lamb, but he had taken Uriah's wife, and that was much more wicked.

Nathan told him this history to show him what a wicked thing he had done.

Nathan said to David, God has been very kind to you, and made you king. Why have you disobeyed his commandments? God will punish you for your wickedness.

NATHAN REBUKING DAVID.

David was very sorry when he heard that God was angry with what he had done, and he said, I have sinned against the Lord.

David was really sorry for what he had done. He was not

like Saul, who only cared for the punishment; he was most sorry because he had displeased God.

He asked God in his psalm to wash out his sins. These were some of David's words: Wash me, and I shall be whiter than snow. Create in me a clean heart, O God! and renew a right spirit within me.

You see that David prayed to God to forgive him, and God did forgive him; yet still, God would punish David, that all people might know that God hated wickedness.

PLANTING RICE IN THE EAST.

CHAPTER LV.

DAVID, OR THE PUNISHMENT.

God said he would punish David, though he had forgiven him.

David had a great many children. I cannot tell you about all his children, but I will tell you of one called Absalom. He was a very proud young man, handsome, had beautiful hair, and was very vain of his beauty; he also told lies, and even killed one of his brothers who had offended him. When David heard how Absalom had killed his brother, he was angry with him for a long time, and would not see him; but at last he let him come to his palace, and kissed him, and forgave him. David ought never to have allowed Absalom to come to Jerusalem again after he had killed his brother; but David was too fond of Absalom.

Yet Absalom did not love his father David. He wished to be king instead of David, and so he behaved very kindly to all the people in Jerusalem, that they might love him better than they loved his father, and make him king. He used sometimes to kiss the poor people that he saw, and tell them that if he were king he would be very kind to them.

This kind way of behaving made the people love Absalom, for they thought that he really cared for them.

When Absalom saw that many of the people loved him, he asked David's leave to go from Jerusalem into the country. David did not know what a wicked plan Absalom had made.

Absalom had directed a great many men to wait till they

KING DAVID FORGIVING ABSALOM.

heard the sound of a trumpet, and when they heard it, to cry out, Absalom is king. So, when Absalom had left Jerusalem, and come into the country, he desired the trumpet to be blown, and a great many of the people called out, Absalom is king!

David was in Jerusalem, and a messenger came and told him that Absalom had made himself king.

He could not bear to think that his son was so wicked as to make himself king. Then David thought of his own sin, and felt that he deserved to be punished. He knew that it was God that let all these things happen to him.

David would not stay in Jerusalem, for he thought that Absalom would soon come there, and would perhaps kill him and his servants. So the king left his palace on Mount Zion, to go a great way off. There were many people in Jerusalem who loved David, and went with him.

They crossed a little river that was outside Jerusalem, and as they went all the people wept.

Then David and his servants went up a high hill, and David wept as he went up, and covered his head. He wore no shoes on his feet: he did these things to show he was unhappy, and all the people with him did the same. You see how much the people loved David.

And when David came to the top of a hill he prayed to God.

Then he went on his journey. Soon he met a very wicked man who hated him, and who called David very bad names, and even threw stones at David and his soldiers. This wicked man called David a child of the devil, and said, You killed Saul, and his children, and now God is punishing you for your wickedness.

At last David and his men came to a place where they rested, for they were very tired. David and his soldiers traveled a long way. At last they crossed over the river Jordan. On the other side there was a place called a wilderness.

There were three very rich men who lived near the wilderness, and who heard of David and his men coming; and these rich men said, They must be very hungry and thirsty, and weary in the wilderness; so they brought David and his men a great many things: beds to rest their weary limbs, cups to drink out of, corn, vegetables, honey, and sheep to eat. These rich men were very kind.

David asked God to comfort him. He felt that he deserved to be punished.

CHAPTER LVI.

DAVID, OR THE OAK TREE.

David lived in a city that had walls and gates.

Absalom soon heard where David was, and came after him with a great army. Absalom crossed over the river Jordan, while his men set up their tents near the city where David was.

Then David saw that his wicked son meant to fight. So David one morning directed his soldiers to go out of the city. David was going with them; but they begged him not to come, lest he should be killed in battle. These people loved him very much. Then the king said, I will do as you think best. David did not wish to go to this battle, for he did not like to fight against Absalom.

David told the soldiers, before they went, not to hurt Absalom; for David still loved his wicked son.

Absalom and his soldiers came out to fight against David's men. They fought in a wood. This was not a good place for fighting, for a great many people were knocked against the trees, and bruised, and killed.

David's men conquered, because God helped them, and Absalom's men tried to run away.

Absalom rode upon a mule—which is a beast very much like a horse. As he was riding, he passed under a great oak tree, and his beautiful long hair was caught in the boughs; and the mule ran away, and left him hanging by the hair in the tree, with his feet lifted up from the earth. One of David's soldiers saw him, and went to the captain, and said, I saw

DAVID GOING TO HIS CHAMBER.

Absalom hanging to an oak. Then Joab said, Why did you not kill him? If you had, I would have given you a great deal of silver, and some clothes. But the man answered, If you would have given me a thousand pieces of silver, I would not have

DEATH OF ABSALOM.

hurt Absalom, for I heard the king desire that no one should hurt him.

When Absalom was dead, Joab blew a trumpet to call back his soldiers; for, now Absalom was dead, the Israelites might leave off fighting. Absalom's soldiers went back to their tents, . and Joab took his soldiers back to the city where David was.

But before they went two men ran to tell David what had happened.

David sat near the gates inside the city. A man stood upon the wall near the gate, to watch whether any person was coming. Soon the watchman saw a man running. Then said David, No doubt he brings some message. Soon afterward the watchman saw another man running. Then David said, He also brings a message.

Soon the first man came up, and cried out, All is well.

He said all was well, because David's men had won the battle. Then the king said, Is the young man Absalom safe? The messenger knew that Absalom was dead, but he did not like to grieve David by telling him this sad news; so he said, There was a good deal of noise and confusion when Joab sent me here.

Soon the other man came running up to David, and said, God has punished the wicked people who fought against the king. Then the king said, Is the young man Absalom safe?

And the messenger answered, May all people who fight against the king be as Absalom now is. The king knew then that Absalom was dead. How very unhappy he was when he heard this. He went into a room that was near the gate, and wept, and said, "O my son Absalom! my son, my son Absalom! Would God I had died for thee!"

When David's soldiers came back, they heard how the king grieved for Absalom, and they felt unhappy, because they loved the king. The king did not come out to meet them, and to thank them for having gained the battle.

CHAPTER LVII.

DAVID, OR THE FAREWELL.

Absalom was dead, David could now return to Jerusalem. The people who had said that Absalom was king now wished David to be king again.

SOLOMON ANOINTED KING.

David was very glad to come back to Jerusalem, because he wished to worship God near his ark, and to hear all the people praising God.

One of David's sons was good. God loved him, and made him good. His name was Solomon. God told David that he was to be king after him. At last David grew very old and weak, and he knew that he should die. So he wished to make Solomon king before he died. He told the high priest to pour oil upon his head; and so the high priest anointed Solomon to be king.

Then David called his people together to a place in Jerusalem, and spoke to all before he died. The king stood up, and said, I once wished to build a house for the ark of God; but God would not let me build a house, because I had fought so many battles, but said that my son should build it.

Then David spoke to Solomon and said, My son, serve God, and He will bless you. Then David showed Solomon the things for building the house: gold, silver, iron, stones, and wood.

Then David prayed to God, and thanked Him for letting Solomon build Him a house, and for letting the people give their things to God. And David asked God to make Solomon love Him, and obey Him. David offered a great many sacrifices to God. Soon after David died.

CHAPTER LVIII.

SOLOMON, OR THE WISE CHOICE.

Almost the first thing Solomon did when he became king, was to offer sacrifices to God.

The night after Solomon had offered the sacrifices, God spoke to him while he was asleep, and said, Ask what I shall give thee.

Now Solomon had just been made king, and he saw what a hard thing it was to be a good king; for Solomon would judge the people: people who quarreled with each other would come to Solomon; and it is very hard, when people quarrel, to find out who is in fault, and who ought to be punished.

Solomon wished very much to judge the people well; and so he asked God to make him very wise.

Solomon said to God, Thou hast made me a king over a great many people, and I am very young; and I do not know what I ought to do. Make me very wise, that I may judge the people well.

God was very much pleased with Solomon, and said, You did not ask me to make you rich, or make you live a long while, or make you conquer your enemies, but you asked for wisdom; therefore I will make you wiser than any man that ever lived; and I will make you very rich too; so that no other king shall be as rich, or as great as you; and if you love me, and serve me as David did, I will make you live a long while.

Then Solomon woke. How pleased he must have been to think of the promises that God had made him. He went back to Jerusalem, and offered up more sacrifices near the ark.

Now I will tell you of something that happened, which showed that God had made Solomon as wise as He said He would.

One day there came two women to Solomon. They had quarreled with each other. Solomon was the judge, and the women stood before him.

One of these women held a dead babe and the other held a living babe. Both the babes were very little creatures, only a few days old, so that the living babe was not old enough to sit up, or to look about it, or to smile.

The woman who held the dead babe seemed very unhappy, and said to the king, This dead babe is not my own child. The other babe is mine. I lived in the same house with that woman, and no one lived in the house but us two; and one night that woman lay upon her child in bed, and killed it; and she got up and put her dead babe into my bed while I was asleep, and took my living babe into hers. When I woke in the morning, I was going to feed my child, but found only this dead child; but when I had looked at it I saw it was not my own child.

Then the other woman said, You do not speak the truth; the living child is mine and the dead one is yours. Then the other woman said again, No, the living child is mine, and the dead one is yours.

Which of these women spoke the truth, and which of them told untruth? How could Solomon find out? How could he tell which ought to have the living babe?

But God had made Solomon very wise, and he thought of a way to find out who spoke the truth.

Solomon called out, Bring me a sword. And the servants brought a sword to the king. Then Solomon said, Cut the living child in two, and give half to one woman, and half to the other; because both the women say the child is theirs, so let them each have half.

Then one of the women cried out, Oh! do not cut the child in two, but let that woman have it; only do not kill it.

But the other woman said, Let the child be cut in two, and let us each have half.

Now which do you think was the mother of the living child? Was it not the one who said, Do not let it be killed?

Solomon knew which was the mother, and he said to his servant, Give her the living child and do not kill it; she is the mother of it.

Why had Solomon desired the man at first to cut the babe in two? Had he intended to have it killed? Oh! no. He only wanted to see what the women would say, that he might find out which was the mother. Was that not a wise plan of Solomon's? God had really made him wise as He had promised He would.

All the Israelites heard of what the king had said to the women, and they were surprised at his wisdom, and were afraid of him.

CHAPTER LIX.

SOLOMON, OR THE TEMPLE.

Solomon should build a house for the Lord.

This house was to be called a temple; and it was to be very beautiful.

BUILDING THE TEMPLE.

Solomon had a great many things to build it of: gold and silver, and iron, and brass, and stones, and wood; and he had a great many servants to build it. David, his father, had told him how to build it.

Solomon did not build the temple upon Mount Zion, but upon another high hill in Jerusalem.

Solomon ordered a great many large stones to be laid upon the ground for the beginning of the house; then he directed his servants to cut down trees. Solomon built the wall and the roof of wood, and covered the inside of the house with gold.

How beautiful the house must have been inside. How bright it must have shone when the candlesticks were lighted.

At last the temple was quite finished, and it was the most beautiful house in the world.

It could not be moved about as the tabernacle had been in the wilderness; but Solomon never wished to move it from Jerusalem. It was a great deal larger than the tabernacle.

When it was finished, Solomon sent for all the people to come to the temple. They came, and carried the ark into a little room in the temple, called the Holy of Holies; Solomon had made a great door to the little room, and he had placed a great curtain or veil over the door, and had made two very large cherubim, or angels, of wood covered with gold, and had placed them in the little room. The large cherubim stood upright, and each had two great wings stretched out all across the little room. The priests left the ark under the wings of the great cherubim, and no one could see into the little room because of the great door, and the curtain.

The other part of the temple was filled with priests, and with singers all clothed in white, and holding harps and other

DANIEL IN THE LION'S DEN.

kinds of musical instruments in their hands—and some of the priests blew trumpets. These were the words the singers sung:

"Oh! give thanks unto the Lord; for He is good, for His mercy endureth forever."

As soon as the priests had left the ark in the little room, and while the priests and singers were praising the Lord in the temple, the Lord Himself came down in a cloud, and filled the temple so that the priests and singers were obliged to go out of the temple, and to stand in the court.

How glad Solomon was to see that the Lord had come into the house that he had built for Him. Solomon liked to see the brightness of the Lord.

Solomon had made a high place of brass; and put it near the brass altar in the court, and stood upon this high place, so that all the people could see him.

And Solomon knelt down on this place, and spread wide his arms, and began to pray to God. His prayer was very long; but I will only tell you a small part of it. He asked God to hear all people who were unhappy and who were sorry for their sins, and to forgive them.

When Solomon had ended his prayer, there came down fire from heaven, and burned up the beasts that had been killed and spread upon the altar. The fire did not hurt the people; it only burned the dead beasts on the altar.

When the people saw the fire, and the glory of God, they bowed themselves down to the ground, and praised the Lord, and said, He is good; His mercy endureth forever.

At last the people went home to their own houses, but they very often came to offer sacrifices at the temple, and to pray to God.

SOLOMON'S THRONE.

CHAPTER LX.

SOLOMON, OR THE QUEEN'S VISIT.

You remember how God once spoke to Solomon in the night, and how He let him choose what he would have.

A long while afterward God spoke to Solomon again in the night.

God said, I have heard your prayer and if you obey me as David did, I will bless you; but if you do wicked things, and worship idols, then I shall be very angry, and this beautiful house that you have built shall be thrown down.

Solomon was very rich and very wise, as God had promised. He built a great many ships, a palace, and a great many towns; and he made a great throne with six steps all covered with gold, and images of two lions on each of the steps, a lion on each side, and a seat at the top for himself.

When Solomon spoke, he said such wise things that people came from a great way off to hear him, and brought him presents; some brought cups of gold or silver, and some brought clothes, and others brought spices, and some brought horses and mules.

So Solomon grew very rich. He sent his ships to far countries over the sea, and they came back full of gold, silver, and ivory. Solomon was the richest king in the world.

I told you that people came from far countries to hear him say wise things, for Solomon knew a great deal: he knew all about the plants from the highest tree down to the least plant

QUEEN OF SHEBA.

.hat grows; he knew about the beasts, birds, fishes, worms, and insects; but he knew something much better than these things, he knew about God and how to please Him, and he gave people very wise advice.

THE QUEEN OF SHEBA AND SOLOMON.

Now there was a queen who lived a great way off, who heard of Solomon, and how wise he was; and she wished very much to hear him talk, and to see the house he had built.

She had a great many questions to ask him: I believe that her questions were about God. She had not been taught about God in her own country, and she wanted to know a great deal about Him. She was called the queen of Sheba. She was very rich, so she brought a great many servants with her, and a great many camels with spices and gold, as presents.

Solomon was very kind, and answered all the questions that she asked. He showed her all the things he had built. The queen was quite surprised at all she saw and heard, and said to king Solomon, How happy are your servants who are always standing near you, and who hear the wise things you say. Blessed be the Lord your God, who has made you king.

Then she gave a great deal of gold and silver to king Solomon, and he gave her all the things that she desired; and then the queen went back with her camels and her servants into her own country.

The queen of Sheba brought back to her own home something better than her presents; she brought a great deal of wisdom in her mind. I hope that she left off worshiping idols, and loved the true God.

A great many of the wise things that Solomon said, are written down in the Bible; they are called "The Proverbs." When you are older, my dear children, I hope you will read them. I think even now you would understand some of them

CHAPTER LXI.

SOLOMON, OR THE IDOLS.

God had appeared to Solomon twice. The first time God promised to make Solomon wise; and the next time to bless him, if he served him.

IDOLATRY OF SOLOMON.

I must now tell you of the wicked things that Solomon did, when he was old.

He married a great many wives. This was wrong. People

might then have had two wives, or a few wives; but God liked best that they should only have one. You remember that Jacob had two wives. If a man now was to have two wives, he would be punished; then he might have two wives, but not so many as Solomon had.

Solomon had seven hundred wives. I think that Solomon had grown proud, and that he wished to be a very grand king, and it was thought very grand for a king to have many wives.

These wives were wicked: they worshiped idols. At last these wives persuaded Solomon to like their idols, and to build altars for the idols on the high places round Jerusalem; and Solomon did even worse than this, he worshiped some of the idols himself. You did not think that he could have been so wicked. He was very foolish to worship idols, which are only made of wood, or stone. Solomon knew what was right, but he did not do it.

God was very angry with Solomon, and said to him, Because you have done this, one of your servants shall make himself king; he shall take away a great deal of the land of Canaan from your son, as soon as you are dead.

I believe Solomon was sorry for his wickedness before he died; but I am not quite sure that he was. It must have made him very sorry to know that God would punish him.

When a king dies, the king's son is king instead of his father. So, when Solomon died, his son was king instead of him; but very soon one of Solomon's servants tried to make himself king. The servant's name was Jer-o-bo-am. This servant made himself the king over a great part of Canaan; but Solomon's son was still king over the rest of the land.

CHAPTER LXII.

JEROBOAM, OR THE DRIED-UP HAND.

Jeroboam made himself king over part of Canaan. Jerusalem was not in Jeroboam's part of Canaan; it was in the part that Solomon's son was king over. It was a good thing for Solomon's son that he had Jerusalem. The temple was in Jerusalem; and in the temple, God came down in a glorious cloud.

You know that God had desired all the people in Canaan to come to Jerusalem very often to worship him. Jeroboam ought to have come to Jerusalem to worship God; but he would not. He was very wicked, and he told his people not to go to Jerusalem.

He did not like to go, because there was another king in Jerusalem. He did not wish his people to go to a place where there was another king, lest they should like the other king best. Then Jeroboam did a very wicked thing: he made two golden calves, and set them up in his part of Canaan, one calf in one town and the other calf in another town. He set up the calves that people might worship them instead of God. He said, Do not go to Jerusalem, it is too far off; worship these golden calves.

Jeroboam worshiped the calves himself. One day God sent a prophet to tell him of his wickedness. Jeroboam was standing by an altar burning incense to a golden calf, when the prophet came, and told him how angry God was with the people who worshiped the golden calves, and how he would punish them. And the prophet said, This is a sign that God is angry; the altar shall be broken and the ashes that are on it shall fall to the ground.

When king Jeroboam heard this he was angry, and he wished to punish the prophet; so he stretched out his hand, and said to his servants, Lay hold on him. Now while Jeroboam's hand was stretched out, God made it grow dry and stiff, so that he could not pull it back; at the same time the altar was broken, and the ashes fell upon the ground, as the prophet had said.

Jeroboam must have been frightened then. He knew that no one could make his hand well but God; so he said to the prophet, Pray thou to the Lord thy God for me, that my hand may be made well.

The prophet prayed to God, and God made the king's hand well.

Then Jeroboam did not try to hurt the prophet any more, because he was afraid; but Jeroboam did not repent of worshiping idols and turn to God; he went on teaching his people to pray to the golden calves. And God was angry with Jeroboam.

CHAPTER LXIII.

ELIJAH, OR THE RAVENS.

Jeroboam was called king of Israel; and Solomon's son was called king of Judah. At last Jeroboam died, and there was another king instead of him; and at last that king died, and then there was another king; and at last he died, and then there was another king, so there were a great many kings, one after the other. I am sorry to say that they were all wicked, and that they all worshiped the golden calves that Jeroboam had made. I will not tell you the names of these kings; and my reason is, I am afraid that you will not remember them. But I will tell you the name of one of them.

At last, after a great many kings had died, one after another, there was a king called Ahab.

He was more wicked than any of the other kings. One of the worst things he did, was to marry a wicked woman who worshiped idols. This woman was the daughter of the king of another country; she had been brought up to worship idols, and she was very fond of idols, and did a great many wicked things. This woman's name was Jezebel.

The name of Jezebel's favorite idol was Baal; and she persuaded Ahab to worship Baal, as well as the golden calves: and Ahab built a temple for Baal in the town where he lived. There were a great many men who used to teach people to worship Baal, and these men were called the prophets of Baal: and Jezebel was very kind to them, but she tried to kill the people who loved God. There were some people in the land of Israel who would not worship Baal.

One very good prophet that lived in the land of Israel was named Elijah: he would not worship idols, and he tried to persuade other people to love the true God. God often spoke

THE RAVENS FEEDING ELIJAH.

to him, and told him what would happen, and Elijah prayed very often to God.

Ahab and Jezebel hated Elijah because he was good, and they would have liked to kill him. Elijah was very sorry to see so many people in the land worshiping Baal; and he wished very much that they should be sorry for their wickedness. At last God sent the people a punishment.

God did not send any rain for a great many months, nor did He let any dew come on the grass in the morning; so the hot sun scorched the grass, and the corn did not grow, and the trees did not bring forth fruit. All the people were very unhappy.

How did Elijah get food when there was no rain? God told him to go to a place where there was a brook, in a secret place, where he might hide himself from Ahab: and God promised to send some ravens to feed him.

So Elijah went to this brook, and he drank of the water of the brook; and in the morning some ravens flew to him, and brought him some bread and meat; and in the evening they came again, and brought him some more bread and meat; and the next day they came again, both morning and evening; so Elijah had breakfast and supper every day, and he wanted nothing more.

Most ravens are wild, but God made these ravens gentle. Elijah must have been glad when he saw them coming with the food. How he must have thanked God for sending them every day.

Elijah lived quite alone by the brook, but he knew that God was with him. After a while there was very little water in the brook; the sun dried up the water, and no rain came to fill it up. At last there was none left.

CHAPTER LXIV.

ELIJAH, OR THE WIDOW.

When the brook was dried up, he told Elijah to go a great way off to a place where a poor widow lived, who would give him food.

Elijah went across the land of Canaan, till he came to a town just outside Canaan. Now the people who lived in this town were heathen, and worshiped idols.

When Elijah came to the gate of the town, he saw a poor woman gathering sticks, and Elijah knew that she was the widow who was to give him food; he called to her, and said, Bring me, I pray thee, a little water in a cup, that I may drink.

I do not wonder that Elijah was thirsty, for he had walked a long way, and there was now very little water in the land of Canaan.

This widow was kind, and started for the water for Elijah. Then he called her again, and said, Bring me, I pray thee, a morsel of bread.

Then the poor widow said, I have no bread; I have only a handful of flour, and a little oil in a jar, and I was just gathering some sticks that I might make a fire, and make the flour and oil into a little cake, that I and my son might eat it; and as we have no more food, when we have eaten it we must die.

Elijah said to the widow, Go and make a little cake for me first, and afterward make one for you and your son; for God has said, that there shall always be flour in your barrel, and oil in your jar, till He sends rain again upon the earth

What a wonderful promise this was. She went and made a fire, and mixed the flour and oil together, and made some bread for Elijah, and then she made some for herself and her son; and still there was flour in the barrel, and oil in the jar; and every day she found enough for them all.

Elijah came and lived with this poor widow; he lived in a room up-stairs. She found it was a good thing to have such a man in the house. Elijah could teach her about God; for you know that she had been brought up to worship idols.

Now you shall hear of a very sad thing that happened to this poor woman. One day her son, who was a little boy, fell sick, and he was so very sick that he died. The poor widow was unhappy. She knew that God had let him die, and she thought that God was angry with her; and she wished that Elijah had not come to her house; so she went to Elijah, and spoke angrily to him. It was very ungrateful in her to behave in this manner. Then Elijah said, Give me thy son.

Now the widow was holding the dead child in her arms, and Elijah took the child in his own arms, and carried him to his own room, and laid him on his bed. Then Elijah began to pray to God. O Lord my God! he said, hast thou made this sad thing happen to the widow?

Then Elijah stretched himsef upon the child, as it lay dead; he did so three times, and he prayed to God, saying, O Lord, my God! I pray thee let this child's soul come into him again.

And the Lord heard Elijah's prayer, and let the child's soul come into him again, and then the child was alive. Then it was warm, and it breathed.

ELIJAH RESTORING THE WIDOW'S CHILD.

Elijah took the child in his arms, and brought him down stairs, and gave him to his mother, and said, See, thy son is alive. Was she angry now with Elijah? Oh no. Now, said she, I see that you are a man of God, and all that you tell me about God is true.

CHAPTER LXV.

ELIJAH, OR THE TWO ALTARS.

Elijah lived a long while with the poor widow. Ahab and Jezebel, the wicked king and queen, did not know where he was. They would have been glad to find him. Ahab sent to all the countries round; but no one could find him. Ahab was angry with Elijah because Elijah had told Ahab that God was angry with him for worshiping idols.

The Israelites were very unhappy because they had so little food; even king Ahab had not grass enough in his fields for his horses, so that a great many of them died.

Elijah was sorry for the Israelites, and prayed to God to send rain, that more corn and grass might grow. God heard this prayer, and he told Elijah that he would send rain; but first he told Elijah to go and show himself to king Ahab.

Elijah did what God told him; for he knew that God would take care of him. So Elijah left the widow and her son, and set out on a long journey. I think that the widow must have been sorry when Elijah went, he had fed her and taught her about God; but God had promised to make her flour and oil last till he sent rain.

Now while Elijah was on his way to king Ahab, he met a good servant of Ahab's.

This servant was looking for grass for king Ahab's horses. The servant knew Elijah.

Then Elijah said, Go and tell king Ahab, that I am here.

The servant was afraid, for he thought that while he was gone to tell Ahab, God would take away Elijah, and that Ahab would be angry and kill him. Ahab was a cruel master, and his servant was afraid of making him angry.

But Elijah promised that he would stay till Ahab came, so the servant believed Elijah's promise, and went to look for Ahab.

His servant told him that Elijah was waiting to see him. So Ahab came to the place.

When Ahab saw Elijah, he spoke angrily, and said, Are you the man that troubles the people of Israel?

Ahab thought it was Elijah who had asked God not to let the rain come.

Then Elijah said to Ahab, It is not I that trouble the people of Israel. It is you that have made these troubles come by your wickedness. You have not obeyed God, and you have worshiped Baal.

Then Elijah told Ahab to get all the prophets of Baal together, and send them to him on a very high hill.

Would Ahab do what Elijah had asked? Yes, because he wanted rain, and he thought that Elijah could ask God to send it.

One morning very early Elijah was on the high mountain with Baal's wicked prophets, and a great many people were standing all round; and king Ahab was there.

Elijah wanted them to see that his God was the true God; so he said to them, Let Baal's prophets take a bullock and kill it, and lay it on the altar, and then let them ask Baal to send fire from heaven to burn up the bullock. I will take another bullock and kill it, and lay it on the altar. I will ask the Lord to send fire from heaven; and if Baal send fire, then you will know that He is the true God; but if my God send fire, then you will know that He is the true God.

The people liked what Elijah said, and they answered, It is well spoken.

Then Elijah told Baal's prophets to take their bullock first. So they took it and killed it, and put it on the altar with some wood; but they put no fire to the wood. Then they began to pray to their god to send fire. They cried, O Baal, hear us. They went on calling out, O Baal! hear us, till twelve o'clock; and they jumped about the altar, as they used to do when they prayed to him.

At last Elijah said to them, Cry louder. Perhaps your god is talking, or perhaps he is hunting, or perhaps he is taking a journey, or perhaps he is asleep, and you must wake him.

Was Elijah in earnest? Oh! no; he knew that Baal was nothing at all: only those foolish people said that there was a god called Baal.

Still the prophets of Baal went on praying for fire; and at last they cut themselves with knives, and made blood flow, because they thought it would please Baal; they thought he was a cruel god that liked their blood. So they went on till three o'clock n the afternoon; but no fire came from heaven.

Then Elijah said it was time to ask his God to send fire; so Elijah built an altar with twelve stones, and laid some wood on the altar and laid the bullock on the wood; and then he desired the people to throw twelve barrels of water over the altar. There was a river just at the bottom of the hill. Elijah made a ditch all around the altar, and this ditch was quite filled with water, and the altar was wet.

Elijah wished the water to be poured over the sacrifice, to show the people that he had not hid any fire in the altar, or near it; for if he had, the water would have put it out.

DEATH OF THE PRIESTS OF BAAL.

All the people were standing round, while he prayed before the altar.

This is what he said: Lord God of Abraham, of Isaac, and of Jacob, let it be known this day that Thou art God, and that I am Thy servant.

And God heard Elijah. Fire came from heaven, and burnt up the bullock and the altar; yes, the fire burnt the stones, and even the water that was in the ditch.

How surprised the people were at this sight. They fell on their faces and said, The Lord He is the God.

Now they saw that Baal was not the true God. So Elijah desired the people to take hold of the wicked prophets of Baal, and to bring them down to the river at the bottom of the hill, and to kill them with swords. These prophets had taught the people to worship Baal, so God chose that they should die.

Did the people leave off worshiping Baal? We shall soon hear what they did.

RUTH.

ELIJAH'S SERVANT SEEING THE CLOUD.

CHAPTER LXVI.

ELIJAH, OR THE RAIN.

You have heard how the prophets of Baal were killed. Now Elijah knew that God would soon send rain; so he told Ahab that there would soon be rain, and that he might go and eat and drink. But Elijah did not eat and drink. He went up to the top of the hill to pray. He threw himself upon the earth, and bent down his head very low.

Elijah told his servant to stand up while he himself was praying, and to look a great way off over the sea, and to tell him what he saw. Do you know what Elijah wished his servant to see? Elijah wanted God to send clouds in the sky, that there might be rain. The servant went up and looked and said, There is nothing. Then Elijah told him to go and look seven times. The seventh time the servant came and said, I saw a little cloud a great way off, as big as a man's hand.

Elijah knew that God had heard his prayer, and that the cloud would grow larger, and that rain would soon come down. So he told the servant to tell Ahab to get ready his chariot and horses, and to drive fast to his own house, which was a great way off; for that there would soon be a great rain.

So Ahab rode in his chariot with his horses, and God made Elijah so strong that he ran faster than the horses, and got first to the city where Ahab lived. While Ahab was driving, and Elijah was running, there were a great many clouds in the sky, and soon there was a great rain.

How glad the people were when the rain came down. It

"ELIJAH IN THE WILDERNESS."

filled the dried-up ponds, refreshed the withered grass, and softened the hard ground. Now the people knew that more corn and grass would soon grow in the fields.

When Ahab got to his own city where he lived, he found the queen Jezebel there, and he told her all that had happened: he told her how Baal did not send fire from heaven, and how God did; and he told her how Elijah had killed the prophets of Baal.

Jezebel was very angry with Elijah, and she sent a man to tell him that she would kill him the next day.

When Elijah heard that Jezebel wished to kill him, he was afraid, and would not stay in the city where she lived; but he went very quickly all through the land of Canaan, till he came to a great wilderness. He did not take his servant with him, but went there alone. In the wilderness there were trees and hills, but very few houses and people.

Elijah was quite alone. He sat down under a tree, and prayed to God to let him die. He was afraid that Jezebel would kill him; but he was more unhappy because Jezebel went on in her wickedness. After Elijah had prayed, he lay down under the tree, and went to sleep. Soon some one touched him. It was an angel. The angel said, Arise and eat.

Then Elijah looked, and saw a fire, and some bread near it that had just been baked; and a jug of water was close to his head. Who could have got ready the bread and the water? It must have been the angel. So you see that an angel was his servant. God sends his angels to wait upon people who love Him. They fly down quickly from heaven, when God tells them to.

Elijah ate and drank the bread and water, and then lay down again, and slept. But soon the angel woke him again, and said, Arise and eat, for you will soon walk a great way.

So Elijah ate and drank again, and afterward walked a great way in the wilderness; but the angel's food had made him strong, and he lived without eating and drinking for forty days.

SOLOMON'S WISE CHOICE.

CHAPTER LXVII.

ELIJAH, OR THE CALL OF ELISHA.

Elijah walked forty days in the wilderness, till at last he came to a mountain. There he found a cave; and he went in and slept. While here, God spoke, and asked him why he had come there.

Then Elijah said, The people of Israel have thrown down God's altars, and killed God's prophets, and I am the only one left; and they try to kill me.

Then God told him to come out of the cave. Elijah came out, and stood upon the mountain. And God made a very great wind blow, that tore the mountain; then he made the mountain shake, and fire come. How dreadful it must have been to see and hear these things. But God wanted to show Elijah how strong He was; so he might know that God could take care of him, and punish wicked people who tried to hurt him. Then God spoke to Elijah in a gentle voice, and when he heard his voice, he covered his face with his cloak, and went and stood inside the cave.

God asked Elijah again wny he came there, and Elijah told the Lord again that the people were wicked, and that they wanted to kill him.

Then God told Elijah that He would soon punish the wicked people for worshiping idols; and God said that all the people did not worship Baal; and that there were a great many in Israel who had never bowed their knees to Baal.

ELIJAH, OR THE CALL OF ELISHA.

God told Elijah to go and find a man called Elisha, and anoint him prophet.

Then Elijah left the cave, and went to look for Elisha. At last he came to a field where a man was plowing. There were

ELIJAH PASSED BY HIM.

twenty-four oxen drawing the plow. They were harnessed two and two; and each pair had a great piece of wood over their necks, called a yoke. A man was walking by the side of the last oxen. This man's name was Elisha.

Elijah came up to the man, and taking off his own cloak,

threw it over the other's shoulders. Why did he throw the cloak over the man? He wished to show him that he was to come with him; and the man knew what Elijah meant. He left his oxen, and ran after Elijah, and said, I will come with thee; only let me first go and kiss my father and mother.

A HIGH PRIEST.

CHAPTER LXVIII.

ELIJAH, OR THE VINEYARD OF NABOTH.

I am going to tell you of a very wicked thing that Ahab did. He was very rich. He had two houses. One of his houses as in one town, and the other was in another town. Near one of these houses there was a garden full of vines. A garden of vines is called a vineyard. This vineyard was close to Ahab's house, and belonged to a man called Naboth. Ahab wished very much to have this vineyard. So Ahab said to Naboth, If you will give me your vineyard, I will give you a better one instead, or I will give you some money for it.

But Naboth answered, No; my father gave it to me, and I do not choose to sell it.

Ahab was angry, because he could not get the vineyard, and went home to his other house. He was so unhappy that he lay down and turned away his face, and would not eat any bread.

Ahab was foolish to be unhappy about a vineyard. He had a great many beautiful things, yet he wanted more.

Jezebel saw how unhappy Ahab seemed, and she went to him, and said, What makes you so sad?

And Ahab said, I asked Naboth to sell me his vineyard, and he said, "I will not sell it."

Then Jezebel said, Are you not a king? Do not be unhappy: eat and drink; I will give you the vineyard.

Jezebel had a wicked plan in her mind—she meant to have Naboth killed! So she wrote some letters to some wicked

JEZEBEL LOOKING OUT ON JEHU.

NABOTH'S VINEYARD.

judges who lived near Naboth, and told them to get some other wicked people to say that they had heard Naboth say very wicked words against God and the king; and then to order people to kill him for it.

Then Jezebel sent these wicked letters to the judges in the town where Naboth lived. When they had read them, they did as she told them. They desired two men to say that they had heard Naboth say very wicked words against God and the king. And then the judges said that Naboth must be killed; and the people took him out of the city, and threw great stones at him till he died. God saw the blood of Naboth, and was very angry with the wicked Jezebel, who had ordered him to be killed; and God was angry with Ahab too, because he had allowed Jezebel to write the letters.

Jezebel said to Ahab, Go, and take the vineyard of Naboth; for he is not alive but dead. Then Ahab went where the vineyard was, to take it for his own.

God spoke to Elijah, and said, Go to the vineyard where Ahab is, and tell him that dogs shall one day lick his blood.

So Elijah went to the vineyard.

I am glad to tell you that Ahab was frightened at the message, and was very unhappy. If Ahab had not cared for what God had said, God would have been still more angry with him.

A long while afterward, Ahab went to fight a battle against some people who lived near Canaan. Ahab went to the battle in a chariot drawn by horses. A man there shot an arrow into his body, and the blood began to flow out. The driver of the chariot took Ahab back to the land of Canaan, and as Ahab was on the way, he died.

CHAPTER LXIX.

ELIJAH, OR THE THREE CAPTAINS.

When Ahab was dead, there was another king. He was one of Ahab's sons, and his name was A-ha-zi-ah. He was wicked like his father Ahab, and his mother Jezebel. He worshiped idols too.

After he had been king a little while, he met with a dreadful accident. He was in a room upstairs, and fell out of the window. He thought that perhaps he should die, and he wanted very much to know whether he would get well. Ahaziah was so foolish that he thought an idol could tell whether he should die or live. So he sent his servants a great way off, to an idol.

As the servants were going to the idol, they met a man, but did not know who he was. This man was dressed in the skins of beasts with the hair outside, and he wore round his waist a piece of leather called a girdle. It was Elijah. God had told him to speak to the servants of king Ahaziah.

Elijah told the servants that God was angry with Ahaziah for sending to an idol to know whether he should get well; and that he should surely die.

How surprised the servants must have been when they found that the man they met knew where they were going, and what the king's message was. They did not go on to the idol's house, but they went back to tell Ahaziah what the prophet had said. He said to the servants, What sort of a man was he?

And the servants said, He wore clothes covered with hair, and a leathern girdle.

Then Ahaziah said, It is Elijah.

Ahaziah was very angry with Elijah for having said that he should die, and he wanted to see him; but he knew that Elijah could do wonders, so he determined to send a great many men to find Elijah, and to make him come. So he ordered a captain to take fifty soldiers with him, and to go and bring Elijah.

The captain found Elijah sitting on the top of a hill; and the captain spoke to him in a rude manner, and said, Thou man of God, the king hath said, Come down.

Elijah said, If I be a man of God, then let fire come down from heaven, and burn up you and your fifty men. And the fire came down from heaven, and burned up the captain and his fifty men.

Ahaziah found that the captain and the soldiers did not come back. Then Ahaziah sent another captain with fifty soldiers; and this captain found Elijah on the top of the hill; and he said, O man of God! thus hath the king said, Come down quickly. You see that this captain spoke even more rudely than the other captain had done, for he said, Come down quickly.

And Elijah answered, If I be a man of God, let fire come down from heaven, and burn you up and your fifty men. And the fire of God came down from heaven, and burned them up. So these soldiers never returned to king Ahaziah.

Then he sent another captain and fifty other soldiers. Now this captain had heard what had happened to the other captains. What could this poor captain do? The king would have been very angry if he had said he would not go. This is what the captain did. He went to Elijah, and behaved in a very humble manner. He threw himself down upon his knees and begged Elijah to spare his life. The angel of the Lord said to Elijah, Go down with him; be not afraid.

So Elijah went with this captain to the king.

Elijah found Ahaziah lying sick in bed, and he told him that because he had sent to ask the idol whether he should get well, God would let him die.

Very soon afterward king Ahaziah died, and there was another king instead of him, and he was wicked.

CHAPTER LXX.

ELIJAH, OR THE CHARIOT OF FIRE.

Elijah once wished to die. But God chose that he should never die, but go up to heaven without dying. When Elijah knew that he was soon going up into heaven, he went to a great many places where his friends lived.

I think they must have felt sorry to part with him; only they knew that he was going to be happy.

Elisha wished very much to see Elijah go up to heaven, so he determined to keep close to him. Elijah said, Pray stay at this place, while I go to another place, where the Lord has told me to go.

And Elisha said, I will not leave thee.

Soon afterward Elijah said, Stay at this place while I go on.

No, said Elisha, I will not leave thee.

Soon Elijah said again, Stay at this place while I go on.

No, said Elisha, I will not leave thee.

So Elijah and Elisha walked a great way together from place to place. At last they came to the river Jordan. Then Elijah took off his cloak, and folded it up, and struck the waters with it; and God made a path through the waters, and Elijah and Elisha walked through the river on dry ground.

After they were gone over the river, Elijah said to Elisha, Ask what I shall do for thee before I be taken.

Elisha wished to be such a prophet as Elijah was, so he asked for a great deal of his spirit. He did not want people to praise him; he wanted them to praise God.

ELIJAH TAKEN UP IN THE CHARIOT.

Elijah said, You have asked a hard thing, but if you see me when I am taken, it shall be so; but if not, it shall not be so.

They still walked on, and talked to each other. I think they talked of God, and of heaven, and of what they could do to please God.

As they were talking, there came down from heaven a chariot, and horses of fire—that is, angels, who are bright like the fire—and Elijah was taken away from Elisha, and carried up into heaven: and Elisha cried out, My father, my father!

Elisha loved Elijah as if he had been his father; for he had taught him about God. As Elijah was taken away, his cloak fell from him, and Elisha picked it up, and when he came back to the river Jordan, he struck the waters with it as Elijah had done, and the waters went up on each side, and there was a dry path, and Elisha walked over alone.

Then Elisha saw that God had made him such a prophet as Elijah had been. Some of Elijah's friends were standing on the other side of the river, and they saw the wonder that Elisha had done, and they said, The spirit of Elijah is in Elisha. And they came, and bowed themselves down to him.

Now Elisha began to go about from place to place, as Elijah had once done, and teach people about God, and do wonders, to show people that his God was the true God.

CHAPTER LXXI.

ELISHA, OR THE BEARS.

People who loved God loved Elisha, but wicked people hated him. There were some people who even laughed at him; there were even some little children who dared to mock him. I will tell you about these children.

People who have no hair, or only a little hair, on their heads, are called bald. Elisha was bald. One day Elisha came near a town where a great many people lived, who worshiped idols. Little children came out and met Elisha; they mocked him, and said, Go up, thou bald head. They told Elisha to go up to heaven as Elijah had done, that they might not see him any more.

Elisha turned, and said that God would send them a dreadful punishment.

The children soon found that Elisha had spoken truth; for two bears came out of the wood, and tore forty-two of these children into pieces.

No doubt the children tried to run away, when they saw the bears coming, but it was of no use; they could not escape.

You have now heard what became of wicked children who mocked Elisha, and you shall hear next of his kindness to a poor woman who had lost her husband. Her husband had been a good prophet, but poor, and had not been able to pay for all the things he had bought.

The woman came to Elisha and said, My husband is dead,

and I cannot pay my debts. A man is come to take away my two sons to be slaves.

The woman was very unhappy at the thought of losing her dear boys. Elisha was sorry and said, What hast thou in the house?

And the woman said, I have nothing but one pot of oil. Sweet oil was used for food.

Elisha said, Go and borrow a great many empty cups, jugs, and basins, and bring them into thy house, and shut the door upon thee and thy sons, and pour the oil into all these cups and basins, and put them by.

The woman knew that Elisha could do miracles, because God was with him to help him, so did as Elisha had told her.

She poured, and poured, and still there was oil left in her pot. At last she said to her son, Bring me another cup. But he said, There is no more. So she went to Elisha, and he said, Go and sell your oil, and pay your debt; and when the debt is paid, keep all the money that is over to buy bread for yourself and your children.

CHAPTER LXXII.

ELISHA, OR THE LITTLE ROOM.

Elisha used to go from place to place to teach people about God.

There was one very rich lady who used to ask Elisha to come in.

This kind woman wished that she had a room for Elisha to sleep in, and she said to her husband, Let us make a little room close to our house; and let us put in it a bed, a table, a stool, and a candlestick, that Elisha may sleep in it when he comes this way.

And the lady's husband allowed her to have such a little room built. Soon afterward Elisha came that way, and slept in the room. Elisha must have liked it very much—he could sit there alone, and think of God; he could write because there was a table, and when it was dark he could light the candle, and go on writing or reading.

Elisha thought the woman had been very kind to make a room for him, and he wished to do something to please her, for he was grateful: he was very kind to people who were kind to him. Now Elisha had a servant called Gehazi. Elisha told Gehazi to ask the woman to come to him. And she came. Elisha thanked her for her kindness and asked whether she would like to have him speak to the king about her, so that the king might take notice of her.

Then the woman said, No, she would rather stay where she

was. So Elisha said to Gehazi, What shall I do for her? And Gehazi said, She has no child.

Gehazi thought that she would like to have a little child. Then Elisha told Gehazi to call her again, and she came, and stood at the door. And Elisha said, Next year you shall have a son.

The woman was very much surprised to hear this, and could hardly believe it. Next year she had a son. She was very fond of him indeed. She thought it was very kind in God to give him to her.

One day when the child was grown old enough to talk, he went out with his father into a field where men were reaping; for his father had a great many fields full of grain. It was morning, yet the sun was hot, and the child soon cried out, My head, my head! The child felt such a pain in his head, that he could not stay in the field.

So the father said to one of his servants, Carry him to his mother. The servant carried him home to his mother, and he sat on her knees till twelve o'clock, and then died. Oh! how sad the mother was, when she found her little boy was dead.

The mother went into the room she had made for Elisha, and laid him on his bed, and shut the door. Elisha lived at a place a great way off, and the lady wished very much to go and see him. She asked her husband to allow her to have one of the servants go with her, and one of the horses for her to ride upon, that she might go to Elisha. And her husband said, Why do you want to go to Elisha to-day? This is not the Sabbath day. Because Elisha used to teach people about God on the Sabbath day.

DEATH OF THE WOMAN'S CHILD.

And the woman said, It shall be well. But she did not tell him why she wanted to go; I suppose she was afraid of grieving him. A servant went with the lady, and she said to the servant, Go quickly and do not stop, unless I tell you.

At last they came to the hill where Elisha was. He was with his servant Gehazi; and he saw the woman coming, while she was a great way off, and he wanted to know why she was coming to him so quickly, for he thought that something was the matter. So he said to Gehazi, Run now to meet her, and say, Is it well with thee? Is it well with thy husband? Is it well with thy child?

So Gehazi ran, and asked the woman. And she said, It is well. She knew that it was well, or right, because God had made her child die. Yet the poor lady felt very unhappy.

When she came up to Elisha, she got off her horse and threw her arms round Elisha's feet. Gehazi was going to thrust her away. But Elisha would not let him do so, but said, Let her alone; she is very unhappy, and God has not told me what has happened to her.

Then the woman said to Elisha, Did I ask you for a son?

Then Elisha saw that her son was dead. So he gave his own staff or stick to Gehazi, and told him to go quickly, and to lay the staff upon the face of the child.

Gehazi went and laid the staff on the child's face, but the child remained quite dead. So Gehazi went and met Elisha coming, and said, The child is not awakened.

At last Elisha came to the house. He went into his own little room, and found the child lying dead on the bed; he shut the door, and prayed to God to make him alive again; and then lay upon the child, putting his mouth upon the child's mouth, and his eyes upon the child's eyes, and his hands upon the child's hands, and the child's flesh began to grow warm. Soon the child sneezed seven times, and then opened his eyes.

ELISHA RESTORING THE SON TO HIS MOTHER.

Then Elisha called Gehazi, and desired him to go and tell the woman to come. When she came into the room, Elisha said Take up thy son. Before she took up the child, she fell at Elisha's feet, and bowed herself to the ground, and then she took up her child, and went out of the room.

Elijah once made a widow's child alive again; and now Elisha made a child alive; for Elisha was such a prophet as Elijah had been, and could do wonders like him. God had promised that he should be like Elijah, if he saw him taken up to heaven; and God kept his promise.

ISLAND OF RHODA-NILE.

THE FLIGHT INTO EGYPT.

CHAPTER LXXIII.

ELISHA, OR THE LITTLE MAID.

There were a great many heathen people lived outside the land of Canaan. You know that people who worship idols, are called "heathen." Some of these heathen people used often to come into Canaan, and rob them.

Once some of those heathen people came, and took away a little girl; and they sold her for a slave to wait on a rich lady in a country a great way off. The lady's husband was called Naaman. He was a great captain, and could fight well in battle.

But Naaman was very unhappy, for he had a dreadful disease called the leprosy. He had very sore white places on his body. He could not find anybody who could cure him of his disease. No doctors could cure him; nor could any of the priests of his idols. Now the little girl who waited on his wife had heard of the wonders that Elisha did, and she felt sure that he could cure him, and said, Oh! that my master were with the prophet; for he would cure his leprosy.

Somebody heard what the little girl said, and told Naaman. Naaman wished very much to be made well, and determined to go and ask Elisha to make him well.

Elisha heard that he was coming, and knew God would help him to make Naaman well. He hoped when Namaan was well, he would worship the true God, who could do such wonders; for Elisha did not wish people to praise him, but he wished them to praise God.

Naaman came into Canaan in a fine chariot with horses, and

NAAMAN'S CAPTIVE MAID.

brought a great many servants. He was proud, and he expected that Elisha would pay him respect, because he was so rich. He drove up to the door, but Elisha did not come out to meet him; he only sent a messenger, who said, Go and wash in the river of Jordan seven times; and your flesh shall be well.

Then Naaman was very angry, and said, I thought that the prophet would come out to me, and would have stood, and called on the name of the Lord his God, and struck his hand over the sore place and made me well. Besides being angry at this, Naaman did not like to wash in a river of Canaan; he would rather have washed in one of the fine large rivers of his own country. Naaman was so very angry that he was going home to his own country without washing in Jordan; but his servants came to persuade him to wash in Jordan. They said, If the prophet had desired you to do some very hard thing, would you not have done it, that you might have been made well? Now he tells you to do a very easy thing; only to wash in the river Jordan; and will you not do it?

Naaman listened to what they said; he went to Jordan, and did so seven times, and his flesh grew as soft and smooth as the flesh of a child.

Now Naaman was glad that he had done as Elisha had told him. Where do you think that Naaman went, when he was well? Did he go home immediately to his own country again? Oh! no; that would have been very ungrateful. He went first to Elisha's house, and brought all his servants with him.

He did not feel so proud as he had done before; he did not expect Elisha to come out to him, but he went in; and told him that he was sure his God was the true God, and he promised that he would never worship idols any more.

Naaman wished to give Elisha some money and some beautiful things, as a reward, so he begged him to take some of the things he had brought with him. But Elisha would not take anything. He wished to show Naaman that he had not made him well in order to get money.

Naaman begged Elisha very much to take something; but Elisha still said he would take nothing. You see that Elisha did not care for money.

Then Naaman set out in his chariot to go back to his own country. You remember that Elisha had a servant called Gehazi. Gehazi heard his master Elisha say he would not take anything from Naaman, and Gehazi wished very much that he could get some of the beautiful things himself; so he thought of a way of getting them by telling an untruth.

So Gehazi ran after Naaman's chariot; at last they saw him running, and he stopped the chariot, and got out, for he was afraid that something was the matter. Naaman said, Is all well? And Gehazi said, All is well, but there are two visitors at our house, very good men, who are very poor, and my master would like some silver, and two suits of clothes, to give to them.

This was not true, but Naaman did not know that Gehazi was telling lies; so he gave Gehazi twice as much silver, and put it in two bags, and gave him two suits of clothes.

Then Gehazi went to Elisha's house to wait upon him. He little thought that Elisha knew of his wickedness; but there was

One who saw him. God told Elisha that Gehazi meant to buy vineyards, fields, sheep, oxen, and slaves with the money.

Elisha said to Gehazi, Where do you come from? And Gehazi said, I have not been anywhere. You see that Gehazi told another untruth to hide his wickedness. Then Elisha said, Did not my heart go with thee? Let the leprosy of Naaman be upon thee forever. Immediately sore white places came on Gehazi's skin, and he went out of Elisha's sight. Gehazi could not live with Elisha any more, for people who had the leprosy were obliged to live by themselves.

At last Elisha died. God did not take him up to heaven in a chariot of fire. He died in his bed, and his spirit went to heaven, but his body was buried in the ground. After Elisha was dead, the people of Israel grew still more wicked. King Ahab had been a wicked king, and Ahaziah his son had been wicked; and the next king was wicked; there was another king, and he was wicked; and at last he died, and there was another king, and he was wicked; and there were a great many kings of Israel, one after the other, and they were all wicked. At last God determined to send a great punishment to all the people of Israel.

There was a king who lived a great way off, in a country called Assyria. He was a heathen king, was very rich, and had a great many soldiers. The King of Assyria came with his soldiers into the land of Canaan, and fought against the people, and conquered them; the soldiers got into all their towns, and took away all their things.

This was the punishment God sent them at last, because they would worship idols, and do many wicked things.

CHAPTER LXXIV.

HEZEKIAH, OR THE KING WHO TRUSTED IN GOD.

When Solomon's son died, his son was king of Judah; and when he died, his son was king—and so there were a great many kings, one after another. At last there was a good king

HOUSE ON THE CITY WALLS.

called Hez-e-kiah, who lived at Jerusalem, and liked to worship God in the temple, and he persuaded a great many people to come and worship God; for Hezekiah loved God.

The king of Assyria sent some of his soldiers to Jerusalem; and they brought their tents, and waited all round the city, and tried to get in. The walls around the city were high and strong, and the people shut the gates fast; still they were afraid lest the king of Assyria's soldiers should get in at last. But Hezekiah knew that God could keep them from being hurt. One day the king of Assyria wrote a letter, and sent it to Hezekiah. It was a very wicked letter. He said: Your God cannot save you from the king of Assyria, who has conquered a great many countries: the gods of those people could not save them, neither can your God save you.

Some men brought this letter to king Hezekiah, and he read it. He could not bear to read such wicked words against God; so he took it into the temple, and spread the letter before God, and began to pray. He said, O God! Thou art the true God; Thou hast made heaven and earth. Other gods are only idols, made of wood and stone; they could not keep people from being hurt. Oh! save us from the king of Assyria, that everybody may know that Thou art the only God.

God heard Hezekiah's prayer. He sent that night His angel to kill a great many of the people of Assyria as they lay in their tents. The angel did not kill them all; but the rest were frightened, and went back to their own country.

CHAPTER LXXV.

NEBUCHADNEZZAR, OR THE GOLDEN IMAGE.

At last Hezekiah died, and there was another king; and at last he died, and there was another king; and at last he died, and there was another king; and so there were a great many kings, one after another, and most of them were wicked. Most all the people in Jerusalem were wicked, and worshiped idols. So God sent prophets to tell them that He would not keep them from being hurt any more, and that He would let some heathen king take them a great way off. You remember that the people in the other part of Canaan, who were called the people of Israel, had been taken away by the king of Assyria; and God said that the people of Judah should be taken away by some other king.

At last there came a rich, proud king, called Nebuchadnezzar, to fight against the people in Jerusalem. This king came from a country called Babylon. He had a great many soldiers, who got into the city, broke down the wall, and burnt many houses, and even burnt the beautiful temple that Solomon had built, and took away the golden things he had put in it.

Nebuchadnezzar also took the king that was at Jerusalem, and put out both his eyes, and brought him to Babylon, and kept him in prison till he died. He killed a great many people, and he took a great many more with him to be slaves.

They sat down by the rivers of Babylon, and wept, and they would not sing psalms as they used to do, but they hung their harps upon the willow trees that grew by the water side.

NEBUCHADNEZZAR.

Nebuchadnezzar made a very large image of gold; higher than a tree. This image was placed out of doors, and Nebuchadnezzar sent for all the judges and captains in his land, and for many rich people to come and see it. Nebuchadnezzar had made three young men, who would not worship idols, judges; so they were obliged to come too, to see the golden image. Then they all stood round the image, and a man called out, Oh! people, when the music begins to play, fall down and worship the golden image. Whoever does not fall down and worship, shall immediately be cast into a burning fiery furnace.

EASTERN WAR HORSE.

Very soon the music began to play, and then some men came to Nebuchadnezzar, and said, O king! live forever. There are three men who have not minded what you said: they never worship your gods, nor have they worshiped the golden image you set up.

Then Nebuchadnezzar desired the men to be brought to him. He said, You do not worship the golden image I have set up? Next time the music is played, if you fall down and worship, it is well; but if not, you shall be cast into the furnace, and who is the God that can deliver you out of my hand?

Then the young men answered the king. O Nebuchadnezzar, our God is able to deliver us. But if not, we will not worship the golden image. Then Nebuchadnezzar was full of fury, and ordered the furnace seven times hotter than usual, and had the three young men thrown into the furnace. Then the three young men fell down in the midst of the flames.

The king was astonished to see them walking about the furnace, and a man with them who looked like the Son of God.

Nebuchadnezzar said, I see four men loose, walking in the midst of the fire; and they are not hurt, and one of them is like the Son of God.

Then the king called the young men by their names, and said, Oh! servants of the most high God, come forth. And the three young men came out of the furnace. Then all the judges and captains came near and looked at the young men, and saw that they were not the least hurt, not a hair of their heads were singed, nor were their clothes scorched, nor did they even smell of fire. Nebuchadnezzar saw that there was a God who could deliver his servants from the burning flame; and he said, if any person spoke against God he should be cut to pieces.

www.ingramcontent.com/pod-product-compliance
Lightning Source LLC
Chambersburg PA
CBHW021155230426
43667CB00006B/403